The Star Spangled
BUDDHIST

The Star Spangled
BUDDHIST

Zen, Tibetan, and Soka Gakkai Buddhism
and the Quest for Enlightenment
in America

JEFF OURVAN

Skyhorse Publishing

336 8455

Skyhorse Publishing books may be purchased in bulk at special discounts for sales promotion, corporate gifts, fund-raising, or educational purposes. Special editions can also be created to specifications. For details, contact the Special Sales Department, Skyhorse Publishing, 307 West 36th Street, 11th Floor, New York, NY 10018 or info@skyhorsepublishing.com.

Skyhorse® and Skyhorse Publishing® are registered trademarks of Skyhorse Publishing, Inc.®, a Delaware corporation.

Visit our website at www.skyhorsepublishing.com.

The author gratefully acknowledges permission to reprint the Meal Gatha from the Mountains and Rivers Order, www.mro.org; from the Buddhist Publication Society for use of an excerpt from *Last Days of the Buddha: The Maha Parinibbana Sutta*, by Sister Vajira and F. Story; and from Brian Daizen Victoria for reprinted excerpts from *Zen War Stories*, RoutledgeCurzon, © 2003.

The author is further grateful for the use of lyrics from Leonard Cohen's *Anthem*, © 1992 Stranger Music Inc. All rights administered by Sony/ATV Music Publishing LLC, 8 Music Square West, Nashville, TN 37203. All rights reserved. Used by permission.

10 9 8 7 6 5 4 3 2 1

Library of Congress Cataloging-in-Publication Data

Ourvan, Jeff.
  The star spangled Buddhist : Zen, Tibetan, and Soka Gakkai Buddhism and the quest for enlightenment in America / Jeff Ourvan.
    pages cm
  Includes index.
  ISBN 978-1-62087-639-8 (hardcover : alk. paper) 1. Buddhism–United States. 2. Buddhism and culture–United States. I. Title.
  BQ732.O97 2013
  294.3′920973–dc22

                      2013005416

Printed in the United States of America

In memory of Shin Yatomi and to our eternal friendship

"The purpose of Buddhism is not to produce dupes who blindly follow their leader. It is to produce people of wisdom who can judge right or wrong on their own in the clear mirror of Buddhism."

—Daisaku Ikeda

"The essence of warriorship, or the essence of human bravery, is refusing to give up on anyone or anything."

—Chogyam Trungpa Rinpoche

"Enlightenment is crap. Living ethically and morally is what really matters."

—Brad Warner

CONTENTS

Preface

In 1983, I was a nice, Jewish, macrobiotic geologist who somehow was enlisted to play sousaphone in a Buddhist marching band.

I attended college in the late '70s and early '80s, reading the colorful works of Carlos Castaneda and similarly groovy books like *The Tao of Physics*, which attempted to reconcile theoretical physics and Eastern mysticism, and *Seth Speaks*, which featured an otherworldly being, channeled through a medium, who explained the mysteries of life and death in a tone reminiscent of my kindly uncle from the Bronx. I was ripe, in those days, for an introduction to new philosophies.

Armed with my geology degree, I worked for a year at the Lamont-Doherty Earth Observatory and then left, in a first stab at reinvention, to seek a more meaningful existence in Manhattan—to do something that might concern people more than rocks. But I didn't know what that was just yet, so I bided my time editing physics journals transliterated from Russian in an office building smack in the middle of what was then a rundown Soho neighborhood.

I would have lunch alone, every day, at a nearby restaurant called Souen. The menu was Spartan: a lot of seaweed, tofu, and grains. One July day, a very bright waitress whom I had never seen before was my server. I was shy back then, especially around pretty girls, so I'm sure I wouldn't have shared anything with her about myself other than what I wanted to eat; the lunch itself was bland and routine.

I ate, rose to pay, and weaved my way between the tables to the cash register, but no one was there to help me. My boss at the time was a stickler for punctuality, so I was nervous about being late. I looked around, but my waitress was busy, bustling in and out of the kitchen and serving other wan vegans like me. I stood there and gazed out a large window. With every changing light, the traffic on Sixth Avenue passed by. I checked my watch—I would be late. I leafed through the magazines and flyers on the cash register's counter, but nothing was of interest to read. Then I boosted my feet up off of the floor and myself onto the counter to peer around the other side of the register, where I saw a small alcove with an index card taped to its interior. The card read: "A blue fly, if it clings to the tail of a thoroughbred horse, can travel ten thousand miles, and the green ivy that twines around the tall pine can grow to a thousand feet." I jumped back down, and my waitress came to take my check.

"Who said that?" I asked.

"What?"

Unintentionally, I found myself trapped in her large, brown eyes. "The blue fly thing."

"Nichiren! Nichiren Daishonin!"

I had heard of Kant and even read a bit of Marx and Engels, but I didn't know what she was talking about. "Nietzsche?"

"No. This is Buddhism." She invited me to a meeting the next evening.

I didn't know what to think, or whether it would even be safe to attend a small meeting of an unknown religion at some strange person's East Village apartment. So I asked around until I found someone in my weekly Tai Chi class who knew what it was all about. Apparently, so I was told, everyone lies down in the dark, holds hands, and chants. And for some reason, I found that to be appealing.

I showed up the next evening at a walk-up leading to one of those old New York so-called railroad apartments in which you enter through a narrow vestibule, and proceed through a tiny kitchen, a small bedroom, and into a slightly larger main room. A group of people were on their knees on the floor there, with their backs to me, facing a closed, wooden box on the wall. I couldn't see anyone's face but heard an unusual, incessant sound:

Nnnnnrrrrrrrrrrrrrrrrr......

I thought there was an audiotape in the box on the wall from which this strange tonal vibration emanated. It wasn't until I sat on the rug, having been welcomed by my waitress, Grete, that I realized this was the collective noise of people chanting *Nam-myoho-renge-kyo*. It was the first time I had ever heard such a sound.

The meeting had nothing to do with holding hands in the dark. Rather, the group recited a portion of the Lotus Sutra and chanted to a paper scroll with Chinese markings inside of the now-opened box.

The people were unusual, too. As a flannel-shirted scientist, I suppose I led somewhat of a narrow life up to that point: The most distinguishing feature among most of my white, tectonically inclined male friends was whether or not one had grown a beard. I was raised in the northeast Bronx, in a large, state-subsidized housing development called Co-op City, so I wasn't utterly sheltered. But in this roomful of about twenty Buddhists I saw what was for me an infrequent gathering: a gay couple, several African Americans, a Puerto Rican group leader and half a dozen incredibly beautiful women.

Most of the women, I learned during the discussion part of the meeting, were friends with a successful fashion photographer and occasional *Penthouse* magazine studio shoot director who was also very adept at introducing his subjects to this particular Buddhist group. I was twenty-one years old and single—their presence was definitely something of interest to me, whether it specifically pertained to Buddhism or not.

But of all the experiences I had that night, I vividly recall a testimonial by an African American woman, whom I never again saw after this meeting. She looked right at me and insisted that if I wanted to change my life then this was the practice for me.

I wish I could say that I immediately took to studying some of the key concepts of Buddhism—the Ten Worlds, the Nine Consciousnesses, the Eightfold Path, the Four Noble Truths, the Three Jewels, and dependent origination—but all that came much, much later. What attracted me at first was the promise of change. Moreover, the Buddhist view that life and the workings of the universe are themselves grounded in a paradigm of cause and effect held great appeal to me as a would-be geologist. Imagine: a religion consistent with modern science!

The half-dozen supermodels that surrounded me at the end of the meeting and coaxed me into joining their group had everything else to do with me signing, that night, on the bottom line. I was a member now of their Buddhist organization, the Soka Gakkai International, and a week later found myself at a temple in Queens to receive my very own prayer scroll, known as a Gohonzon.

Grete came to my home to help enshrine the Gohonzon in a shirt box I had tacked to a wall. When we started to chant, she advised me to pray for anything I wanted. I prayed, among other things, for a new job, one that would allow me to contribute some good to society. My telephone rang after about five minutes of chanting. A friend of my mother's was on the phone, and she had called to tell me about an opening for a press secretary at a New York City Council office in which she worked. Whether or not this job would actually help people, and whether I even was qualified, were arguable, but that was an impressive display of cause and effect. I applied for the position and got it.

Thereafter, I threw myself into my newfound Buddhist practice and joined in the special activities organized for young men, which, at the time, were held night after night after night. In particular, I signed up for a brass band for which I learned to play tuba. The band was a peculiar mix of professional musicians and utter neophytes like me, but we had a strong spirit, which we attributed to our Buddhist practice. For years we marched down Fifth Avenue as a centerpiece of the annual Columbus Day Parade. I'm still not certain what our participation had to do with either Italian-American civic pride or with Buddhism, but, as far as I was concerned, this was Buddhism in America. And it was fun.

Life, in general, was fun. To the extent I kept chanting, good things kept happening. I had great jobs, and I had a cute blonde girlfriend. Everyone clapped and cheered when I shared my experiences at Buddhist meetings. I had a vision for happiness in the world, and I had a sound philosophy by which peace actually could be secured. As long as I kept practicing my faith, my life was joyful and my future assured. I studied Buddhism and was convinced that I got it. If nothing else, the benefits I received were actual proof.

I later found out that I was mistaken.

It's not that I stopped chanting, or that I felt my Buddhist practice ceased to work, but it's rather that all of the marvelous things that were happening to me no longer fell into my lap. I had problems with my girlfriend, challenges at my job, issues with my health and—suddenly—big questions about the purpose of my life and my faith. Wasn't Buddhism about becoming *happy*? If so, why wasn't I happy? Wasn't it about gaining *benefit*? If so, where did all my lovely benefits go?

My friends in Zen and Tibetan Buddhist groups had a remarkably different take on the objectives of Buddhist practice. To them, it concerned *emptiness* and *wakefulness*, rather than happiness and benefit. At first, I was confused that the approaches to what I thought was simply "Buddhism" were so varied. And then I realized that I didn't comprehend any of it: I already knew that I understood little about Zen and Tibetan Buddhism, but what came as a shock to me was that, after a few years of Buddhist practice, I still didn't even get the point of what the Soka Gakkai was all about.

I used to have a dreamy image that Buddhism would somehow, someday, sweep across America and that everyone would become happy and our society would be at peace. Part of me still holds on to that idealistic notion, but it's tempered now with a keen understanding that such a quest is grounded only on a battlefield of intense personal struggle, individual by individual, spreading out in rippling waves as each person overcomes his or her internal struggles and "lesser self."

This sort of individualized Buddhist quest for enlightenment in America is more romantic than my earlier, quixotic view. And, as revealed in the following pages, it's dramatic, everlasting, and real.

Introduction:
Nirvana Unplugged:
Buddhism in America
Today

The United States is the first, and perhaps only, country in the world in which every Buddhist sect is represented.

Although the exact number of practitioners of any religion is a slippery thing to measure, most reports indicate that between three to four million Americans identify as Buddhists. Among this group, about two-thirds—an estimated two million people of non-Asian descent—consider themselves to be practicing Buddhists. Moreover, hundreds of thousands of Americans of various faiths read about Buddhism, are interested in its philosophical tenets, and tend to view themselves as Buddhists—for example, the many self-described "Jewish Buddhists" or "Protestant Buddhists." They are part of a growing number of Americans dissatisfied with traditional religious offerings, stressed by unrelenting change, and thirsty for an approach to spirituality grounded in logic and consistent with scientific knowledge. Although there are hundreds of sects, or different interpretive schools, of Buddhism worldwide, three primary movements have taken firm root in the United States: Zen Buddhism, Tibetan Buddhism, and Soka Gakkai International (the "SGI" or "SGI-USA").[1]

---

1. A fourth American Buddhist movement inspired by Theravada teachings is known as Vipassanā, or Vipassanā meditation. It's focused on the use of mindfulness meditation to gain insight into impermanence, and its better-known teachers include Jack Kornfield, Sharon Salzberg, and Joseph Goldstein, among others. It's not yet nearly as popular in the United States as Zen, Tibetan, or Soka Gakkai Buddhism and is not a subject of this book.

The practices of these schools are based on the belief that all people are capable of attaining enlightenment—variously defined as an egoless state of life free of delusion, in which an individual is fully awakened and lives without fear, with the ability to have compassion for all beings and a desire to create value in an engaged relationship with society at large. But the differences are also profound: the spectrum of philosophical expression among these three American Buddhist schools is as varied as that observed between Reform, Orthodox, and Hasidic Judaism.

Accordingly, there's no clear popular understanding about what it means to be a Buddhist in America. Are all Buddhists vegetarian? No. Do they all worship images of the Buddha as a divine being? Definitely not. Do all Buddhists employ the method of meditation to achieve enlightenment? Surprisingly, no again. In fact, some of the key teachings of the Zen and SGI schools, in particular, often stray relatively far away from those of Shakyamuni—the historical Buddha, also known as Siddhartha Gautama or the Tathagata, who lived and taught in India some six hundred years before the advent of Jesus Christ.

Buddhism is not a religion in the Western sense but rather a practical set of ideas and approaches toward understanding the workings of life. To be more precise, it's a system of practices and philosophical tenets designed to help people overcome their sufferings. It is to the soul what weightlifting is for muscles—it strengthens the self to the extent that a person's spirit, through devoted practice, becomes impervious to external influences. And it's open and available to everyone.

D.T. Suzuki, a twentieth-century Zen master, first introduced the concepts of Zen to a wide audience in the West in the 1950s. Alan Watts, author of the seminal 1957 work *The Way of Zen*, was one of the first popular Western proponents of the faith and published books on the subject as early as 1936. Bestselling novels, such as Jack Keroauc's *The Dharma Bums*, as well as the writings of Allen Ginsburg and Gary Snyder, brought Zen and Tibetan Buddhist concepts to an even larger readership. The voluminous, recent works of the Dalai Lama and Thich Nhat Hanh have further disseminated Buddhist teachings to an extent to which at least a generalized understanding of Buddhism is now ubiquitous in the United States. Moreover, all the American Buddhist schools have attracted a literate and relatively affluent following with considerable numbers of celebrity practitioners. For example, members of the

SGI include jazz musician Herbie Hancock, rock star Tina Turner, and actor Orlando Bloom; Tibetan Buddhism counts Richard Gere, Steven Seagal, and composer Philip Glass as followers; proponents of Zen Buddhism include Snyder, singer Leonard Cohen and late Apple founder Steve Jobs.

For all their differences, though, the Buddhist schools in America still share some basic, common concepts. Each espouses nonviolence. Each one recognizes the impermanence of life. Each places great importance on a mentor-student relationship. And each upholds the central primacy of what is known in Buddhism as The Three Jewels.

Buddhism and God

Buddhism is not a monotheistic religion, and Shakyamuni is not regarded as a god. He was a common mortal, just like the rest of us. Buddhism doesn't affirmatively deny the existence of God, in the Judeo-Christian sense. It's simply just not a concept that factors into its cosmology.

Buddhism is more aptly described as a study of life. Its practices, especially as expressed in the predominant American Buddhist schools, are concerned with ego, emptiness, wakefulness, happiness, and enlightenment in this lifetime. Whether or not there's a God is treated as irrelevant to this quest. And although questions concerning the afterlife are critical to most schools of Buddhism and developed in a context of profound philosophical detail, such inquiries aren't framed from the Western heaven-or-hell perspective.

Zen, in particular, co-abides with the monotheistic faiths. And whereas Tibetan Buddhism presents a variety of deities and mythical, mystical beings, and Soka Gakkai members offer gratitude in prayer to *shoten zenjin*—protective forces that permeate all existence—these are, for the most part, metaphorical figures not meant to be taken literally. Accordingly, Zen, Tibetan, and Soka Gakkai Buddhism are neither monotheistic nor even polytheistic faiths.

You can go on believing or not believing in God as you see fit. He, She, or They do not enter the Buddhist equation.

Nonviolence

Most conspicuously, Buddhism is a practice of peace. The often voluminous sutras—or sermons—of Shakyamuni contain no justifications for the use of violence. Unlike, for example, certain passages in the Old Testament or the Koran, there are no exceptions carved out in the traditional Buddhist canon rationalizing the use of any violent means toward any end. Buddhists who do take up arms generally have no religious, textual, or philosophical defense based on faith.

But Buddhists, of course, are human. And human nature, at its animalistic depths, can be violent. Accordingly, throughout history, there have been plenty of instances of organized Buddhist violence. These include ancient wars among Chinese monks stretching as far back as a millennium; the support, whether overt or tacit, by several Japanese Buddhist schools of that nation's State Shinto government during World War II; and today's reported display or use of weapons by monks in Thailand and in other parts of Southeast Asia.

A sincere practice of Buddhism, however, inevitably leads toward an elevation of the condition of a practitioner's life so that his or her aggressive or hostile tendencies can be transformed into empathetic ones. Over the past forty years, Buddhists in Tibet have offered spectacular and incredibly brave examples of the application of Buddhist compassion and nonviolence in response to the violent takeover and cultural suppression of their country, and the attempted dismantling of their religious teachings and organizations, by the government of China. Thousands of them have lost their lives as a result. The "engaged" Buddhism of the Zen master Thich Nhat Hanh helped to bring peace and security to Vietnam. And the resistance to State Shinto presented by the founders of the Soka Gakkai stands in stark contrast to the capitulation to state authority offered by other Japanese Buddhist sects in the 1930s and '40s.

Such a pacifist path is by no means passive. Whereas any rational person would, of course, seek to defend him- or herself, it takes a special sort of guts, wisdom, and self-control to not lash out when attacked. Buddhism has a long history of both standing up to authority and compromising before it. Those who stood up when the opportunity arose practiced, with their lives, the right spirit of the philosophy as it is taught.

In general, Zen, Tibetan, and Soka Gakkai Buddhist practitioners in the United States must be considered to be among the most peace-loving Americans today. And while individual political opinions, of course, will run the full spectrum from left to right—and, indeed, there's even a Buddhist

Military Sangha serving active U.S. service men and women—it's not likely to find much, if any, war-mongering among any of these American Buddhist communities.

The fundamental emphasis on compassion that Buddhism teaches derives from the notion shared by all of the American Buddhist schools that every person has within an enlightened Buddha nature. Although there are many interpretations and poetic representations of "Buddha nature," essentially it means that each person, without exception, is already a Buddha and has within them the potential to manifest this highest condition of life. Each of the schools differs greatly with respect to how to practically go about bringing out this Buddha nature, but all agree that it's there.

A helpful method toward understanding, from an introductory perspective, how Buddhism views the conditions of life was developed by the sixth-century Buddhist monk and Lotus Sutra scholar Zhiyi, also known as Chih-i or T'ien-T'ai. He first categorized a system of viewing the human experience through the perspective of "Ten Worlds." These worlds, from highest to lowest, are:

- *BUDDHAHOOD: Enlightenment—a condition of life free from delusion and fear.*
- *BODHISATTVA: A condition of life filled with compassion for others.*
- *REALIZATION: The inherent ability to perceive the true nature of phenomena.*
- *LEARNING: A condition of life in which one aspires to enlightenment.*
- *RAPTURE: A state of life experienced when desires are fulfilled.*
- *TRANQUILITY: A peaceful state of life characterized by the ability to reason.*
- *ANGER: A state of life consumed by the need to dominate others—often accompanied by a pretense of being good or wise.*
- *ANIMALITY: An instinctual state of life characterized by fearing the strong and bullying the weak.*
- *HUNGER: A state of life governed by deluded cravings or desires that are impossible to fulfill.*
- *HELL: A condition of seemingly powerless despair, in which one is trapped in overwhelming suffering.*

The idea is that each person has a predominant state of life corresponding to one of these worlds. But these aren't fixed conditions—people, throughout their lives, will migrate up or down the scale. Many tend to cycle between the lower six worlds, with the occasional glimpse of Rapture the most anyone can really hope for.

Still, Buddhism takes an optimistic view of life on Earth. A person in Hell can make their way out to also experience Buddhahood—it's a matter of sparking one's courage and nurturing one's inherent wisdom about the true nature of life. For example, three people trapped in a stuck elevator can experience vastly different reactions. One might panic—a state of Hell. Another will realize that they, eventually, will be rescued—a state of Tranquility. And the third person, acting out of compassion, may feel compelled to help calm and comfort his or her panicked companion—a state of Bodhisattva.

In Buddhism, as in physics, every effect arises from a cause. The cumulative effect of a person's thoughts and actions is his or her karma. This recognition of and adherence to the concept of cause and effect is the foundation of Buddhist morality. Karma does not imply fate or destiny, however. Buddhists believe that a person's karma can change if the causes he or she makes also change.

One Buddhist sutra states:

If you want to understand the causes that existed in the past, look at the results as they are manifested in the present. And if you want to understand what results will be manifested in the future, look at the causes that exist in the present.

Life, for a Buddhist, is sacred. The act of violence, whether against oneself or others, creates, like every other act, both a cause and an effect. From the perspective of the aggressor, a violent act is rooted in the lowest of the Ten Worlds. Accordingly, a Buddhist will seek to exert his or her self-control in order to avoid making a deeply negative cause. If nothing else, that originating negative cause will boomerang back to the aggressor. The corresponding effect may not necessarily mirror any single cause, but the effect, in the words of the thirteenth-century Japanese Buddhist monk Nichiren, eventually will manifest "as surely as an arrow aimed at the earth cannot miss the target." No matter what that other person may have done or not done to deserve or not deserve retribution or physical punishment, the acting out in a violent way by one against another denies the Buddha nature inherent in both actors' lives.

From a Buddhist perspective, the self-centered and insecure "hard shell of the lesser self," as expressed by Daisaku Ikeda of the Soka Gakkai, is the root of such chronic social problems as racism, sexism, and violence. In contrast, Buddhists view the workings of life and all phenomena through the framework of dependent origination, or what Thich Nhat Hanh has called Interdependent Co-Arising. Put simply, dependent origination means that everything in the universe, including all life, is interconnected. Nothing exists in isolation. In fact, all beings and phenomena exist only because of their relationship with other beings or phenomena. Shakyamuni used the image of two bundles of reeds to demonstrate this principle. Each can remain standing as long as both lean against one another. An awareness of our interconnectedness is essential to all schools of Buddhism.

In fact, such interconnectedness extends even to the self or to our respective ego. Indeed, the concept of self, according to Buddhism, is itself a delusion. In reality, we are in no way separate from others, even though our spirits, egos, personalities, or respective Buddha natures appear to be contained within our individual bodies.

With an understanding of Buddha nature, cause and effect, and dependent origination, of which all are key Buddhist concepts, the path of non-violence is the only one a true Buddhist of any denomination can walk with head held high.

This is no intellectual exercise. The practice of Buddhism will provide any sincere practitioner with the courage and wisdom to triumph over the "lesser self."

Impermanence

Buddhists recognize that neither any phenomenon nor condition of life is permanent.

The universe expands and contracts. The sun—which itself, like all stars, has a life cycle—rises, and then it sets. Plate tectonics proves that earth is both created through volcanic activity and subsumed into magma in seismically active, deep-water ocean trenches. And while the Pacific Ocean incrementally shrinks, the Atlantic grows larger. Seasons change. Water evaporates, and then it rains. The healthy become sick, and the young grow old. We live, and then we die. Flowers bloom, and then they scatter. Every cell in our body declines and is replaced within seven-year cycles. Atomic particles are in constant flux. An exchange of energy and electrons occurs in the simple act of shaking someone's hand. Perhaps matter itself cannot be destroyed, but its form always changes.

Most Buddhists understand Shakyamuni's teachings to emphasize an understanding of the impermanence of all phenomena in order to free themselves from the sufferings that arise from the attachment to things— lovers, material possessions, power—that the passage of time will either destroy or render meaningless. Shakyamuni stated, "I teach one thing, and one thing only: suffering and the end of suffering."

We suffer because we cling to what we love—this is, in Buddhist terms, the First Noble Truth. Moreover, in Buddhist terminology, such suffering is caused by attachment to the "three poisons" of ignorance (or stupidity), greed, and hate (or anger). Such a view is common to all Buddhist schools.

The approach that each of the current major American Buddhist groups takes to impermanence, and the role it plays in their respective *dharma*, or teaching, differs. For Tibetan Buddhists, this teaching of the Buddha compels practitioners to renounce an attachment to this life. In the words of the Dalai Lama, "detaching yourself from the bonds of this life is valuable and useful, while the contrary is harmful. If we were to die this evening, we could prepare ourselves for this passage; and if we were to continue living, all the better. In any case, our preparation will not have been in vain."

A Zen Buddhist, with his or her key emphases on meditation and living in the present moment, would view the contemplation of impermanence as the very heart of his or her practice. In fact, the impermanence of things would be viewed by a Zen Buddhist as a cause for joy and a way to see all of life as a thing of beauty.

Soka Gakkai Buddhists take a somewhat contrary view. While they acknowledge Shakyamuni's teachings with respect to the evanescence of life, an SGI member views the Buddha nature as permanent throughout the existences of life or death. Accordingly, rather than stressing impermanence and the consequent need to eliminate earthly desires and attachments, the Soka Gakkai asserts the ultimate reality of the Buddha nature inherent in all life and encourages active engagement with others and with society as the essence itself of Buddhist practice.

Mentor and Student

Zen, Tibetan, and Soka Gakkai Buddhists all adhere to the Buddhist tradition of mentor and student, or master and disciple. This relationship dates back to the earliest days of Buddhism, during which Shakyamuni's teachings, it is believed, were orally communicated for some 500 years before they were ever recorded in writing.

Although there are many anecdotes, particularly in Zen literature, of mentors berating, hitting, or otherwise physically harming their students, master and disciple is not master and slave. Here's the difference: In a master-slave relationship, the slave exists to support the master and must do his bidding under threat of violence. In a master-disciple relationship, the master exists to support the disciple and might very occasionally speak or act out in a strict manner in order to awaken the disciple to the error of his or her practice.

In the Zen and Tibetan traditions, a student would choose a more senior practitioner—typically a monastic—and request to become his or her disciple. In the Zen community, in particular, the mentor will never ask a student to study with him or her; rather, it's always incumbent upon the student to seek out the relationship. And, as a rabbi might do when a non-Jewish individual requests to convert, the mentor will typically reject the student's advance. The mentor may feel that the student has not yet adequately progressed in faith, or he or she may simply look to test that student's commitment. Whatever the reasoning behind such initial rejection, at its heart the mentor views the relationship as a lifelong endeavor. The student, in other words, had better be prepared to embark upon what will be a lifelong pledge to practice assiduously and search for enlightenment, come what may. A student need not necessarily commit to joining the clergy—in fact, there's a great importance placed on a student laity both within the Zen and Tibetan communities. But in the quest for enlightenment in both of these schools, the leadership of and the relationship with a Buddhist mentor is supreme.

The same holds for the Soka Gakkai, but in this case, there's no need to seek out a mentor. Rather, there already is one: Daisaku Ikeda. Ikeda, eighty-five years old at the time of this writing, is the president of the Soka Gakkai International and for more than fifty years the clear driving force behind the spread of this school of Buddhism throughout the world. Newer Soka Gakkai practitioners learn very early on that Ikeda is their mentor. It takes a relatively long time, however, for most new members to come to understand exactly what that means and to embrace it in a meaningful way. Ikeda's Buddhist teachings, largely drawn from his mentor Josei Toda, the Buddhist monk Nichiren, and lessons learned from a great many modern figures from all walks of life and religious backgrounds, are the foundation for SGI members' Buddhist practices.

The Three Jewels

The Three Jewels, variously also known as the Triple Gem or the Three Treasures, are the three most important refuges for all Buddhist practitioners. The Three Jewels represent the Buddha, the dharma, and the sangha—or the community of Buddhist believers.

The Buddha traditionally represents Shakyamuni. However, it can also indicate a student's mentor, who is thought to have either achieved enlightenment or received a life-to-life transmission of enlightenment from the historical Buddha. More esoterically, it can even represent the Buddha nature in general.

This book broadly views the first "Jewel" of the Buddha from a number of perspectives—including the life of Shakyamuni; the founding historical monastics of the Zen, Tibetan, and Soka Gakkai schools; and the key individuals who brought the respective teachings to the United States.

The second Jewel—the dharma, which according to the Buddhist scholar Robert Thurman means "to be held"—encapsulates the particular teachings of each of these schools, including all of their practices, methods, virtues, ethics, and differing viewpoints. Such viewpoints are surprisingly varied. Although Zen, Tibetan, and Soka Gakkai Buddhists strive toward enlightenment, Zen seeks to achieve this through "awakening" oneself to the reality of life; Tibetan Buddhists practice to achieve "emptiness"; and the SGI promises "happiness." These are not interchangeable ideas, but rather very different approaches that cause very different effects.

Finally, the third Jewel—the sangha—is the specific community of Buddhists helping each other to practice and achieve enlightenment. It can represent a large community, such as all the Zen, Tibetan, and Soka Gakkai Buddhists, respectively, in the world. In the United States, this number is very difficult to pin down. Maybe the concept of impermanence has something to do with it, but whether a person is a die-hard practicing Buddhist, or someone who thinks he or she thinks like a Buddhist, there is no ceremony akin to a baptism to really know for sure. Still, there are hundreds of Zen centers, hundreds of Tibetan and related Shambhala centers, and more than a hundred SGI centers spread throughout every region of the United States, so the number of practitioners is large and growing.

More specifically, though, sangha refers to a Buddhist's immediate community of believers. For a Zen Buddhist, it would include the students attached to the particular Zen center or monastery he or she is connected to, and it would certainly include those who attend services in the center in which one's mentor practices. For a Tibetan practitioner, his or her sangha generally would be the group of Buddhists that likewise practice together in a region or with a specific mentor. Soka Gakkai Buddhists are organized by neighborhood districts and chapters, and in this regard an SGI member's sangha is also local.

The Three Jewels operate as a sort of check-and-balance system. If a teacher promotes a practice that conflicts with the dharma, then it's incumbent upon the sangha to point that out. If the sangha has ignored the dharma teachings, then the teacher has to strictly, yet compassionately, guide those believers back to the correct path.

While the dharma, which has had some 2,600 years to develop, is generally sound and tested, albeit with many innovations and permutations as it was transmitted to different lands, cultures and times, Buddhism can be easily destroyed by an incorrect teacher posing as a sage, or a community of believers asserting religious authority for self-serving purposes.

Without a healthy relationship between the teachers and their respective communities, Buddhism, which developed for the sake of the happiness of each person, and in opposition to any authority that might crush such spirit, can function in a negative manner akin to any other religion that's gone wrong.

PART One

·

THE FIRST JEWEL:
THE BUDDHA

·

1

Under the Bodhi Tree:
The Drama of Shakyamuni Buddha

As the story has been passed down for some 2,600 years, Shakyamuni, also known as Siddhartha Gautama, or the Buddha, began life as a prince of the Shakya tribe (*Shakyamuni* means "sage of the Shakyas") in what is today modern Lumbini, Nepal. He grew up sometime around 600 B.C. in a household in which he was loved, educated, and provided for in every possible way. He lacked for nothing: He had fine clothes, as much as he wanted to eat, a lavish palace, and beautiful women to choose from. The King, his father, had received a prophecy that young Siddhartha would grow to become either a powerful king or a great spiritual leader. Eager for Siddhartha to succeed him politically, the King overprotected him, as we might say today, surrounding him with the best life had to offer and isolating him from the sufferings of the people outside of the palace gates. Despite such a privileged life, however, Siddhartha wondered why he wasn't happy.

According to what by now sounds a lot like an apocryphal story, Siddhartha one day managed to leave his palatial home and visit a nearby city. There, he discovered the reality of the world and witnessed the four sufferings of birth, sickness, old age, and death. These sufferings—common to all, whether a king or a member of the lowest caste—profoundly troubled him, and he contemplated how they might be overcome. Eventually, most likely in his late twenties, he cut off his hair and renounced his throne, his riches, and, according to most accounts, his wife and young son, and embarked on a spiritual quest.

Of course, his actions may be better understood in the context of his times. The quest for personal enlightenment was a serious, and not unpopular, endeavor in the Indian subcontinent of his day. Groups of ascetics were engaged in that era in Shramana or Vedic Hinduism practices, and these movements ultimately gave rise not only to Buddhism, but also Jainism and Yoga as well. Were Shakyamuni to leave his family in such a manner today, a photo of his son undoubtedly would appear in a tabloid under the headline: SURE, HE'S THE BUDDHA, BUT HE'S BEEN A LOUSY FATHER TO ME! But according to Buddhist tradition, his wife, the queen, and his son, a prince, were well cared for by the Shakya tribe. Moreover, it is said that each of them subsequently attained enlightenment as disciples of his teachings.

For years after the renunciation of his worldly life, Shakyamuni subjected himself to harsh meditative and ascetic practices, most of which were likely associated with Shramana or Jainism. Some of their more elaborate ascetic practices, such as long periods of fasting or living in forests unclothed, were so extreme that Shakyamuni nearly died of starvation and exposure. After years of such study, he came to realize that all he had achieved was illness and self-destruction. He then sat down where he happened to be—under a pipal tree, a descendant of which, the Bodhi Tree, still stands on the spot in today's northern India—and he determined to meditate until he reached enlightenment. Then, after some two weeks of what surely was an intense, embattled, and determined meditation, Shakyamuni awakened to the true nature of life and the law, or dharma, that underlies the processes of life and the universe.

What was this enlightenment? It was, in part, a realization of the endless cycle of birth and death, an awakening to the eternal nature of life spanning past, present, and future.

Shakyamuni's Sutras

Within days, Shakyamuni began to teach and ultimately traveled throughout India. Interestingly, he embraced both men and women, rich and poor, and held that Buddhism was a practice for all people without regard to sex or caste. Over his some fifty years of teaching, Shakyamuni, who lived to be approximately eighty years old, generally presented his philosophy in ways that were most accessible to his audiences: thus, in the sutras, his sermons are often presented by way of parable or in a question-and-answer format. As would be the case with many Buddhist leaders who followed, Shakyamuni's life was far from easy. He often encountered jealousy from leading disciples or intrusions from powerful authorities and was said to have endured nine great persecutions. These included an attempt by his jealous cousin, Devadatta, to kill him by pushing a boulder off of a cliff onto him; a second attempt, at Devadatta's instigation, to crush him under a charging, mad elephant; two false accusations by women that he had impregnated them; and various other indignations, including attempts by envious and disaffected disciples to establish a competing Buddhist order.

These efforts, none of which succeeded, mark the first in a long line of attacks, throughout the centuries and up until the present, on individuals who either taught, or sought to reform, the practice of Buddhism.

Daisaku Ikeda of the Soka Gakkai has observed that Shakyamuni's life "was completely untrammeled from dogma," and that his interactions stressed the importance of dialogue. Moreover, it's clear from each of the innumerable sutras attributed to Shakyamuni that he was a person of profound consideration and compassion. And throughout, the theme of his teachings was how to overcome suffering and become happy in this world.

The multitude of different Buddhist schools found today may in part be attributed to the many years over which Shakyamuni taught, as well as the nature and transmission of his teachings. Only a very few of his disciples would have accompanied Shakyamuni on all his travels. Accordingly, many contemporaneous disciples who accepted his philosophy did so based on the perhaps one or two years they actually heard him teach. On a more mundane plane, think of followers of the Grateful Dead over the years: someone who followed them in the 1970s might not consider a Deadhead from the 1990s to have experienced "the real thing" and hold fast to that view, listening only to tapes from the older period, certain in his or her opinion and belief.

Because Shakymuni's teachings, so long ago, were not contemporaneously recorded but only orally transmitted, different Buddhist orders or practices would be established based on the specific teachings that were heard. Indeed, the so-called First Buddhist Council was convened almost immediately after Shakyamuni's death in response to disagreements over how some of the Buddha's precepts were intended to be carried forward. And it would be

hundreds of years—approximately in the first century B.C.—before the first of
these orally transmitted teachings were finally inscribed, beginning with the
Fourth Buddhist Council, which was held in Sri Lanka and resulted in the
writing on palm leaves of the Theravada Pali Canon. Moreover, the written
sutras we know today were produced not from the perspective of Shakyamuni
himself but from his followers. Accordingly, many sutras begin with the phrase
"Thus I heard," or "This is what I heard."

The Vietnamese Zen teacher Thich Nhat Hanh has pointed out that,
inevitably, certain distortions in the original teachings must have occurred over
such a long period of oral transmission. Further, even Shakyamuni himself, in
his final sermon, the Nirvana Sutra, perceived the confusion that might occur
after his death—he specifically warned future Buddhist sanghas to "rely on
the Law and not upon persons," and to "rely on sutras that are complete and
final and not on those that are not complete and final." It appears from these
statements that the Buddha warned against following monks in the future who
would seek to betray his teachings and noted that many errors are bound to
be introduced after his sutras are transmitted to other countries. But Thich
Nhat Hanh, not to mention several other Buddhist figures from antiquity,
demonstrates that enough of the sutras overlap so that any inconsistency often
can be corrected by comparing and contrasting the sutras and other reliable
scriptures. Nhat Hanh refers to it as stringing precious jewels together to form
a perfect necklace.

The Development of Buddhism throughout Asia

As Buddhism spread after Shakyamuni's death from India to China, the
philosophy would be renewed and reformed over the centuries. The older
traditions are broadly known as Theravada or, historically, Hinayana Buddhism;
the "newer" schools, dating from as far back as the first or second century, are
called Mahayana. In addition, the tantric practices of Buddhism are referred to
as Vajrayana. Zen and Soka Gakkai Buddhism are in the Mahayana traditions,
while Tibetan Buddhism, generally a Vajrayana practice, borrows both from
Theravada and Mahayana traditions. Zen itself is a reform movement that
rejected the formalities of contemporaneous Mahayana sects. And the Soka
Gakkai, a relatively modern phenomenon, grew out of the teachings of the

thirteenth century Japanese monk Nichiren—who, for his part, rejected the earlier teachings of Zen and other Mahayana schools prevalent at the time. So Buddhism, while traditional and conservative in nature, periodically undergoes spasms of revolutionary reform. Often, such periods are stimulated by the transmission of the teaching to new cultures.

Buddhism spread quickly throughout India after Shakyamuni's death, but it didn't rise to prominence as a major religion until embraced by Ashoka the Great in approximately 260 B.C. Ashoka was a fierce conqueror of the Indian subcontinent, and, at first, a pathologically violent and bloodthirsty ruler. He supposedly came to power by throwing the legitimate heir to the throne into a pit of hot coals and by killing 99 of his 100 brothers. He established a torture chamber, contemporaneously known as "hell on earth," for his own harem of women. Ashoka's empire stretched from Afghanistan in the north, to Bangladesh and parts of Burma in the east, to Pakistan and parts of Iran in the west, and included almost the entire Indian subcontinent. After a particularly terrible battle in Kalinga, on the east coast of India, in which more than 100,000 were slaughtered, Ashoka was said to have been made sick by the sight of so much suffering. His reaction to the aftermath of the conquest led him to convert to Buddhism, which subsequently became his state religion.

Ashoka was to Buddhism as Constantine was to Christianity. But Ashoka, in a relatively drastic, non-Constantinian shift, incorporated an official policy of nonviolence—although his armies remained strong enough to deter any potential invaders. Ashoka established freedom of religion throughout his realm, built roads, established schools and universities, instituted a policy of vegetarianism, and even constructed veterinary hospitals. His rule is considered the model of the relationship, at least in south Asia, between Buddhism and the state. Rather than dominating his subjects under the threat of a sword or divine favor, Ashoka secured his legitimacy by seeking the approval of the Buddhist sangha. Such a model still exists today, particularly in Thailand.

Moreover, Ashoka sent missionaries to propagate Buddhism to the north of India and as far as Greece, Egypt, and Rome. Interestingly, some think that it was actually the Greeks who first established the now-ubiquitous, green or gold statues of the Buddha. Such statues had not existed throughout the first several hundred years after Shakyamuni's passing, likely because he never taught that he was divine. But some Greeks, who had established trade routes with India during this time and came to settle in what is today Pakistan, may have adopted Buddhism and then blended their polytheistic views, which incorporated idolatry, into the practices they discovered in south Asia. This practice of venerating a statue of the Buddha not only was merged into many, though not all, schools of Buddhism, but it inspired some of the most exalted art that survives from Asian antiquity. In any event, most Buddhists don't consider Buddha statues to be idols but instead, like a cross, symbols that may be helpful to inspire religious devotion.

Buddhism appears to have entered China in the first century A.D. And while the first translations of scriptures and sutras occurred around 150 A.D., Buddhism did not widely spread until the capture in battle of the sublimely pivotal translator Kumarajiva toward the end of the fourth century.

The National Teacher

Kumarajiva was taken by a Chinese general following a losing battle with the Buddhist kingdom of Kucha, where Kumarajiva lived, on the Silk Road in today's northwestern region of China. According to historians, the battle specifically was waged to capture Kumarajiva, already widely known as a great scholar of Buddhism. The Chinese warlord who captured the scholar, Lü Kuang, was supposed to deliver him to the Emperor Fu-chien. Instead, Lü Kuang declared his own state and imprisoned him for some fifteen years, during which Kumarajiva was said to have learned Chinese. Finally, the scholar was ransomed by the Chinese in 401 A.D. at the age of fifty-five.

Fu-chien had since passed away, but a new Chinese emperor bestowed on Kumarajiva the title of National Teacher, and he set to work translating many important sutras, including the Lotus Sutra, which became central to the Tendai, Nichiren, and Soka Gakkai schools of Buddhism, and the Diamond Sutra, which is not attributed to Shakyamuni but nevertheless held in high regard by Tibetan and Zen Buddhists, among others. As a result of Kumarajiva's efforts, a variety of Buddhist sects based on these sutras began to spread widely throughout the Asian continent.

As with early Christianity and the founding of most great religions, Buddhism was subject to violent and repressive periods throughout its history in China. Shortly after Kumarajiva's death, a fifth-century emperor who was a believer in Taoism persecuted its followers for seven years. In the sixth century, another emperor went after both Buddhism and Taoism: both were outlawed. In the ninth century, again at the instigation of Taoists, Buddhists were harassed and executed. And in the tenth century, more than half of all Buddhist temples in China were destroyed in a state-sanctioned effort. Throughout these periods, priests and nuns were forced to return to secular life or were simply murdered, and unknown numbers of temples, statues and sutra texts were destroyed. More modern Chinese persecutions against Buddhism occurred in the seventeenth century, and another, regrettably, is ongoing today in Tibet.

Although Shakyamuni's teachings ultimately reached Japan, the home of modern Zen and Soka Gakkai Buddhism, around the eighth century, the major teachings of Buddhism in America today ultimately are rooted in the fifth-century work of Kumarajiva, the first translator into Chinese of the teachings of Shakyamuni.

Important Buddhist concepts that Kumarajiva introduced to China, and ultimately to the world, include the Four Noble Truths and the Eightfold Path.

The Four Noble Truths and the Eightfold Path

The Four Noble Truths, which were among the earliest of Shakyamuni's teachings as he emerged from his enlightenment under the Bodhi Tree, are:

1. *The truth of suffering.*
2. *The truth of the origin of suffering.*
3. *The truth that suffering can cease or be overcome.*
4. *The truth of the path leading to the cessation of suffering.*

The first of these truths encompasses more than simply suffering. It is meant to indicate that we will inevitably suffer if we anchor our happiness on external matters. Since things outside of ourselves will always change, we will always be at the mercy of such suffering when we lose them.

The second noble truth relates to the nature of suffering, which is rooted in the craving for things outside of ourselves. Such cravings, in turn, are caused by the Three Poisons of greed, anger, and ignorance.

The third noble truth promises that an individual can overcome such sufferings caused by the Three Poisons if he or she learns how to either detach from or not be swayed by them. This process, or the manifestation of this third noble truth, varies between Buddhist schools.

Finally, the fourth noble truth provides a practical method to overcome suffering. This method, too, differs in terminology between Buddhist schools, but it's generally referred to as the Eightfold Path. According to the Zen and Tibetan Buddhist traditions, the Eightfold Path consists of Right Understanding, Right Thought, Right Speech, Right Action, Right Livelihood, Right Effort, Right Mindfulness, and Right Concentration. These are eight dimensions of human behavior that operate simultaneously and in dependence on one another. The Soka Gakkai embraces a similar but streamlined approach to overcoming suffering, which it refers to as "human revolution." Essentially, adherence to the Eightfold Path, or the road to human revolution, leads a person to transform their sufferings or cravings into a state of higher awareness and happiness. This does not, however, indicate that a person needs to detach him- or herself from all desire or retreat to a mountaintop far away from the vicissitudes of modern society.

The Universal Worthy Sutra, one of Shakyamuni's teachings considered an epilogue to the Lotus Sutra, states: "Without either cutting off earthly desires or separating themselves from the five desires, they [the Buddha's followers] can purify all their senses and wipe away all their offenses." Zhiyi's work known as *Great Concentration and Insight* states: "The ignorance and dust of desires are enlightenment, and the sufferings of birth and death are nirvana."

Thich Nhat Hanh notes that the practice of these eight "Rights" constituting the Eightfold Path allows one to face his or her sufferings and transform them into a state of well-being. Or, in the simple words of Nichiren, "earthly desires are enlightenment." He also refers to the path offered by Buddhism as a "ship to cross the sea of suffering."

How this ship is constructed, though, and how effectively and quickly it sets sail, depends both on one's resolve and the specific teachings of the particular American Buddhist school one chooses to study.

2

Zen and the Art of
American-style Maintenance

In response to the formalization of Buddhist practices and monasteries throughout China, the teachings of Zen first appeared as a reform movement in the sixth century. Its founding is attributed to the monk known as Bodhidharma, although its theoretical inspiration is traced to a lotus flower said to be handed by Shakyamuni to his disciple Mahakasyapa. Zen rejects all of Shakyamuni's sutras out of hand. It was a revolutionary development in Buddhism: Zen holds that Buddhist enlightenment is a process of mind-to-mind transmission and that no written texts are sacred. According to Zen, the first such transmission, which is said to continue unbroken until today, was initiated by Shakyamuni through his act of silently passing that lotus blossom long ago.

The Japanese word, Zen, derives from the Chinese word *Ch'an*, which itself is a transliteration of the Pali word *jhana*, meaning meditation. Zen was, and it remains, a popular yet unorthodox stream of Buddhism with a colorful and often controversial history.

Bodhidharma, the presumed founder of this school, taught that enlightenment is transmitted wordlessly from master to student. Although there is some dispute with respect to whether he actually existed or is a combination of historical figures, Bodhidharma, according to most Buddhist accounts, was the son of a wealthy family from southern India who first entered China in the sixth century. Upon his arrival, a large crowd of people, having learned of this great Buddhist scholar, gathered to hear him preach. Rather than speak, however, Bodhidharma sat down and meditated for many hours. Finally, he stood and walked away in silence. People were upset, word spread, and naturally Bodhidharma was brought to the attention of the Emperor. Thus, a Buddhist rock star was born.

Bodhidharma, as rock star, was more of a punk rocker, however, insulting the Emperor with his impertinent teachings, and he was ultimately tossed out of the palace. He proceeded to the north, crossing the Yangtze River and settling in Luoyang. There he asserted that the Buddhist scriptures and sutras were no more than a tool for reaching enlightenment and ought to be discarded. His attitude is summed up by the famous Zen saying: "The finger pointing to the moon is not the moon." Inevitably, like Shakyamuni and many other great Buddhist figures, he encountered abuse, slander, and beatings. After many years of wandering, meditating, and practicing alone, including nine years in a cave, he was ultimately invited to stay at a Shaolin temple and began to systematize his teachings (and also initiate the close relationship to date between Zen and the martial arts). This famous Zen verse crystallizes his teaching:

A special transmission outside the scriptures,
Not founded upon words and letters,
By pointing directly to Mind.
It lets one see into nature and attain Buddhahood.

Two Japanese monks, Saicho and Kukai, traveled to China toward the end of the eighth century, and Buddhism, which had already taken firm root in Sri Lanka, Korea, and Vietnam, began to flourish in Japan. Saicho established the Tendai school, which was based on the teachings of Zhiyi, and Kukai brought Vajrayana teachings to the capital and gained great influence with the court and the nation's rulers. He established the Shingon sect of Buddhism, which, in the Vajrayana tradition, has much in common with today's Tibetan Buddhist school.

Zen, however, was not established as a separate lineage until Eisai, a Tendai monk, traveled to China in the twelfth century, bringing back with him to Japan not only the teachings of Zen but also, of historical note, green tea. As is seen time and again in Buddhist history, the more established schools of Tendai and Shingon, among others, opposed this new teaching, and Eisai

at times was met with violent confrontations. In 1199, however, Eisai moved
to Kamakura, then the seat of the military shogunate, and his philosophy was
enthusiastically embraced by the ruling class. This was the beginning of a
long history of imperial or governmental favor of Zen. In 1215, Master Dogen,
Eisai's contemporary, and perhaps the most revered Zen master in history,
formally established the Soto school of Zen, with an insistence on intensive
meditation and specific monastic rules. The Rinzai school was introduced
later in the thirteenth century but it did not rise to prominence until it was
reformed by Hakuin Zenji in the eighteenth century. Hakuin, among other
accomplishments, is the author of the famous koan: What is the sound of one
hand clapping?

The differences between the Rinzai and Soto schools in America
are subtle. Both emphasize meditation, or zazen, and both encourage the
contemplation of koans, the unique, seemingly illogical stories or riddles that
appear to outsiders to be utterly perplexing and absurd. Rinzai also has the
historical reputation of being the more aggressive sect—its various masters,
not the least of whom includes Hakuin, are memorable in Zen stories for
their supposed use of caustic language and violent assaults on disciples in
order to help awaken them. Thus we have stories of arms being cut off,
fingers being sliced, cats decapitated, and disciples thrown off of monastery
platforms. Such conspicuous violence, thankfully, is not a hallmark of Zen
in the United States.

Zen continued to enjoy the patronage of Japanese shoguns throughout
the centuries. But after a period during which the influence of Buddhism was
diminished, the Meiji Restoration, which opened Japan to the modern world
in the mid-nineteenth century, established Shinto as a state religion. Both the
Soto and Rinzai schools of Zen again sought influence with the ruling powers
of the time, and ultimately both movements were co-opted under an umbrella
of Japanese nationalism and State Shintoism. This, of course, proved to be a
conflicting issue for the Zen community in general, as its institutions were
compelled to support Japan's various twentieth-century war efforts, including
its clashes with Russia and China and its aggressive entry into World War II.
Following the war, the United States finally was introduced, in a meaningful
way, to Zen.

Zen Comes to America

The great early spokesman for Zen in the United States was the author and professor D.T. Suzuki. In the opening years of the twentieth century, Suzuki had lived in Illinois at the home of the scholar and writer Paul Carus. Carus was assisted by Suzuki in the publication of *The Gospel of Buddha*, one of the very earliest works in the West on Eastern philosophy. After World War II, Suzuki shouldered the task of spreading the teachings of Zen and, more to the point, interpreting it according to his viewpoint for the West. His books, including *An Introduction to Zen Buddhism*, which was published with a foreword by no less than the founder of analytical psychology, Carl Jung, were enthusiastically embraced by scholars in the West—despite their conspicuous pro-Japan themes. Notably, Suzuki held a professorship at Columbia University during the 1950s, which provided him with a significant platform from which to espouse his views.

As a university-educated and -affiliated intellectual, Suzuki appeared to be a trustworthy source of information about Zen. He presented the tenets of the faith in as modern terms as possible, and the fact that he was steeped in Western literature and philosophy made him particularly persuasive. Despite the occasional anti-Western comments throughout his works, Suzuki de-ritualized Zen, making it perhaps more palatable to Americans. A theme throughout his writings is the presentation of Zen as essentially inexplicable. Then, as proof, he offers certain koans or Zen stories that most readers would consider incomprehensible. It was an effective approach, as intellectual Americans reading about this exotic philosophy only thirsted for more.

Thus we find curious statements in Suzuki's works that the Buddha himself ought to be rejected, that the sutras should be treated as "mere waste paper," and that Zen is far from nihilistic because even the idea of having nothing should be discarded. According to Suzuki, Zen wants to live only from within. Logic has little or no value, because it's self-conscious and is thus to be avoided. Similarly, according to Suzuki, Zen abhors ethics, which can be defined as the application of logic to the facts of life. Perhaps this outlook explains, in part, the head-in-the-sand approach Zen (and to some extent Suzuki) adopted during Japan's entry into World War II.

Thich Nhat Hanh

One of the most respected Zen writers, teachers, and peace activists since the 1960s is the Vietnamese monk Thich Nhat Hanh. Of his more than one hundred books, forty have been translated into English, including his best-known work, *The Heart of the Buddha's Teaching*. He resides in France, in his Plum Village Monastery, and has also established monasteries in the United States and Vietnam. He is credited with coining the phrase "engaged Buddhism," which suggests a practice of applying the insights and benefits of Buddhist practice for the greater good of society and the world.

Thien Buddhism, a form of Zen, was introduced to Vietnam in the sixth century, sometime after the period that Bodhidharma taught. It was transmitted to the region by an Indian monk known as Vinitaruci, who had studied with Sengcan, considered the third partriach of Ch'an, or Zen, in China. It is this stream of Buddhism that Thich Nhat Hanh practices.

Nhat Hanh was especially active in anti-war activities in the 1960s, both in the United States and in Vietnam. He describes his position against the war as one based on his love for the Vietnamese people but also on his perception that the Americans fighting there were victims of wrong policies as well. In 1966, he met with Dr. Martin Luther King, Jr., and prevailed on him to publicly take a position against the Vietnam War. Dr. King did so in his famous 1967 speech at Riverside Church, in New York. He also nominated Nhat Hanh for the Nobel Peace Prize, although ultimately no award was made that year.

Perhaps as a result of what the Communist leaders of Vietnam considered to be his ambiguous position, Thich Nhat Hanh was exiled from his country in 1973 and not allowed to return until 2005. His overwhelming view of Buddhism is one of forgiveness, grounded in steadfast confidence and wisdom. His perspective, as expressed in his writings, is one of wonder at the miracle of life and its various permutations and phenomena. Reflecting about a military attack on a Buddhist school in which he was sleeping and almost killed, Nhat Hanh wrote:

If you nourish your hatred and your anger, you burn yourself. Understanding is the only way out. If you understand, you will suffer less, and you will know how to get to the root of injustice. . . . When you are

*a victim of injustice, if you get angry, you will suffer one hundred times
more.*

His engaged Buddhism approach differs considerably from the Zen
that D.T. Suzuki described. Suzuki disdained, at least theoretically, full
engagement in matters of the greater society. Nhat Hanh's syncretized Zen,
rather, is ethical and based on a foundation into which he's introduced elements
of other Mahayana and Theravada Buddhist teachings and even methods from
Western psychology. Whether accurate or not, his public image, somewhat like
that of the Dalai Lama's, reflects the general, or even stereotypical, ideal of
how a Buddhist today is perceived by the West—gentle, pacifist, playful, and
reclusive. In this respect, Nhat Hanh's countenance likely has permeated the
Western mind more than any other one Zen Buddhist individual.

Still, Thich Nhat Hanh's influence on how Zen is interpreted in the
United States is rivaled by several even more colorful characters: Shunryu
Suzuki, Bernard Glassman, Robert Aitken, Philip Kapleau, and John Daido
Loori.

A New American Zen

Shunryu Suzuki (not to be confused with D.T. Suzuki) founded the first Soto
Zen monastery outside of Asia, the Tassajara Zen Mountain Center, as well as
the San Francisco Zen Center, one of the most established Zen organizations in
America. He was the author of *Zen Mind, Beginner's Mind*, considered a seminal
introductory work on Buddhism for Western readers, and he trained several
first-generation American Zen practitioners. Suzuki was keenly interested
in bringing the Zen dharma to a new, American audience, finding that the
practice in Japan, in his opinion, had calcified and become rote. Just prior to his
death in 1971, his dharma heir, the soon-to-be controversial Zentatsu Richard
Baker became the first American abbot of a Zen monastery.

Bernard Glassman is an American Zen *roshi* (or master) born in Brighton
Beach, Brooklyn, to Jewish immigrant parents, and trained professionally as
an aeronautical engineer. One of the very first major figures to take Zen in
unprecedented ethical directions, with a unique American flavor, Glassman in
1982 founded the Greyston Bakery in Yonkers, New York, to help the poor and

the homeless. The Greyston Foundation today has some $20 million in assets and serves more than two thousand area residents in need. His Zen Community of New York rebuilt condemned buildings for new housing for the homeless. Glassman is also known for his street retreats, in which he moved the practice of Zen Buddhism literally into the streets, practicing meditation in public parks and conducting *dokusan*, or guidance sessions, in alleyways. He now leads Zen Peacemakers, a confederation of Zen groups promoting Buddhist-inspired, socially engaged activities. Glassman's interpretation of Zen, obviously, extends far beyond what D.T. Suzuki once described.

Robert Aitken, who died in 2010, was a co-founder in 1959 of Honolulu Diamond Sangha. Another interpreter and pioneer of an American Zen seeking engagement with society, Aitken was a peace activist, environmentalist, gay rights advocate, and a proponent of Native Hawaiians' equal rights.

Philip Kapleau, founder of the Rochester Zen Center in western New York, was the author of another influential book on Zen, *The Three Pillars of Zen*. Kapleau, like Glassman and Aitken, had a profound interest in developing in America a socially engaged Zen, something different and apart from that of its expression in Japan.

And then there is John Daido Loori, a tattooed, Italian-American U.S. Navy veteran from Jersey City not typically named on the short list of American Zen innovators. Daido passed away in 2009 at the age of seventy-eight but not before rendering in yet another unique way Zen Buddhism into an American context. If Glassman can be said to have turned left at the crossroads, Daido went right. Having received dharma transmission from both the Soto and Rinzai sects, Daido established the Mountains and Rivers Order and the Zen Mountain Monastery, in Mount Trempor, New York. He also wrote some twenty books on Buddhism, including *The Eight Gates of Zen*, and was a celebrated nature photographer. As the founding abbot of Zen Mountain, he contributed to this new expression of Zen Buddhism in America by, among other things, instituting at his otherwise traditional monastery the practice of reciting Buddhist liturgy in the English language. The effect is thrilling when performed in a service, with the accompaniment of loud drums, the pace becoming faster and faster as would the rhythm of an accelerating horse. Moreover, the Western listener or participant can readily understand and reflect on the words and meanings of the recited prayer.

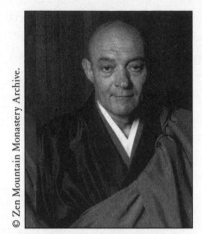

John Daido Loori, founder of the
Mountains and Rivers Order.

From the perspective of practice, and with its emphasis on strict zazen, Zen Mountain is considered to be among the more conservative of Zen monasteries in the United States. Daido himself is recalled as charismatic and fierce, but also gentle, someone who sought "to teach what can't be taught." Although Zen Mountain started as an arts center, Daido and his dharma heirs transformed the group into a traditional monastic community. He instituted clear, ethical, written rules over what once was a fairly libertine group of monastics, including a prohibition on sexual relations amongst themselves.

Daido's approach to Zen is a 24/7 affair: contemplative practices should include not only zazen but everything one does throughout the day, from food preparation to eating and sleeping. His "eight gates" of Zen include zazen, Zen study, academic study, liturgy, right action, art practice, body practice, and work practice. But these aren't intellectual pursuits: these gates require guts and fortitude to enter and thereafter abide without compromise. Where Glassman, in particular, worked in large measure to apply Zen to social endeavors, Daido, also with an eye on doing social good, especially with respect to the natural environment, primarily concentrated on keeping the practice traditional yet as accessible as possible to Americans.

An anecdote is told at the monastery concerning a discussion Daido once had with his teacher, Taizan Maezumi. As the story goes, the younger Daido had grumbled that the Zen practices the older master sought to establish in the United States were "too Japanese" for an American audience. Turning to Daido, his mentor responded: "I am not American, I am Japanese. You change it." Daido, to his credit, opened many leadership opportunities at the monastery to female monastics and offered instruction in uniquely twenty-first-century Western topics, such as gay and lesbian spirituality.

In this sense, Daido, along with Glassman, Aitken, Kapleau and others, was a quintessential American innovator, walking the well-trodden path of American know-how. He took an ancient Buddhist practice and adapted it to become more attractive, productive, and efficient for potential American Buddhist consumers.

3

Tibetan Buddhism:
A Crazy Little Thing Called Wisdom

I n Tibet, a land of beauty, sadness, and poetry, it is believed that the first encounter with Buddhism occurred in the fifth century when a basket of Buddhist scriptures fell from the sky. However they actually arrived, whether by land, sea, or air, it is likely that they came from India, as they were written in Sanskrit. Moreover, it took another several generations before they were finally translated into Tibetan under the reign of a benevolent king, Songtsan Gampo.

As one might expect, the Tibetan Buddhists of antiquity did not have it easy. In the early eighth century, Buddhists from the Chinese city-state of Khotan, one of the world's first Buddhist kingdoms and, at the time, a crossroads through which Buddhism flowed from India to China, fled to Tibet to escape persecution by an anti-Buddhist king. They were protected at first by the Buddhist queen of Tibet, but her sudden death shortly thereafter in what was likely a smallpox epidemic was attributed by adherents of Tibet's nativist Bon religion to her state support of Buddhism. So yet again these refugee Buddhist monks, together with other Tibetan Buddhists, fled, this time to India, where they proceeded to murder one another in a sort of Buddhist internecine civil war.

By the end of that century, however, Buddhism was again established as Tibet's state religion. And at some time during this period, Tibet was visited by the Buddhist sage Padmasambhava—better known as the illustrious Guru Rinpoche, or even sometimes the "Second Buddha"—who thereafter established the unique blend of Theravada, Mahayana and Vajrayana Buddhism recognized today as Tibetan Buddhism.

Guru Rinpoche

According to Tibetan legend, Guru Rinpoche (the "Precious Master") was born intact as an eight-year-old child, preaching Buddhism, while floating on a lotus flower on Danakosha Lake—a mountainous refuge once thought to be the mystical and lost Shambhala, otherwise known as Shangri-La, in today's lawless Afghanistan-Pakistan border. The immaculate child was taken to the local king, who for years had suffered for his queen's failure to bear him a son. The overjoyed king adopted him, named him Padmasambhava ("Lotus Born") and made him heir to a kingdom that encompassed today's treacherous Swat Valley. Presuming at least a grain of truth to this remarkable story, one can't help but wonder how this child actually was procured for the king.

In any event, Guru Rinpoche, like many of the great Buddhist teachers and reformers, soon wore out his welcome and was exiled from the kingdom, purportedly for murdering the son of an evil royal minister. He subsequently traveled for a number of years, preaching and practicing Buddhism in remote cemeteries, curiously, throughout the Indian and Himalayan regions, before finally reaching Tibet.

According to some, Guru Rinpoche was invited to Tibet by its first emperor, Trisong Detsen. Although some accounts state that Guru Rinpoche lived in India for either 3,600 or 1,800 years, more realistic reports state that he spent fifty-five years in Tibet. With the support of the emperor, Guru Rinpoche taught and spread Buddhism throughout the Himalayan regions, persuaded both the people and the rulers to abandon the nativist Bon religion, and established Tibet's first monastery, known as Samye. He is recognized as the patriarch of the Nyingma sect, one of the four major schools of Tibetan Buddhism, and is responsible for the translation of many sutras from Sanskrit to Tibetan. Most importantly, Guru Rinpoche transmitted the Vajrayana teachings to his disciples and is considered the root mentor to all tantric Buddhist masters to this day.

Interestingly, Guru Rinpoche had five female consorts, including Emperor Trisong Detsen's wife. Even more remarkably, he is said to have flown to Bhutan on her back after having transformed her into a flying tigress for the sake of the trip. Together with his consorts, Guru Rinpoche is credited with having eliminated the negative forces of evil mountain deities that affected the people of Tibet and Bhutan at the time.

Guru Rinpoche also is said to have hidden during his lifetime thousands of teachings in caves, forests, and in other remote regions of the Himalayas. These teachings, known as *termas*, were intended for the benefit of future generations. The work known as the *Bardo Thodol*—the *Tibetan Book of the Dead*—is considered to be one of these termas.

The Vajrayana, or tantric method, of Buddhist practice, as taught and passed down by Guru Rinpoche, is something of an extension, or reformation, of Mahayana practices. It did not develop until more than one thousand years after Shakyamuni's death. It is a mystical, ritual-based approach to Buddhism with a primary focus on the transmission of enlightenment from teacher to student. In particular, it seeks to nurture an awareness of the nonduality of life.

The Four Branches of Tibetan Buddhism

In Tibet, apart from the Nyingma school attributed directly to Guru Rinpoche, three other main schools developed over the centuries. These include the Kagyu, Sakya, and Geluk (or Gelug) schools. The Kagyu school emerged in the eleventh century from the teachings of Marpa and his student Milarepa. Milarepa, one of the many bad boys of Tibetan Buddhism, studied sorcery early in his life, which he used to settle a grudge against his aunt and uncle by creating a vicious hailstorm that killed thirty-five members of their family. In a quest to expiate this sin, Milarepa sought out the Buddhist teacher and translator Marpa. After years of meditation and study with Marpa, Milarepa learned numerous esoteric skills, including an exceedingly fast method of running known as wind meditation. He is often depicted in paintings as having green skin, an aspect he developed in life due to his devotion to drinking nettle tea. The tantric school he established is known for a system of meditation and practice called *mahamudra*, which, in general, contemplates emptiness.

In the context of Buddhism, emptiness, which is critical to Tibetan Buddhism, is not to be confused with nothingness. Rather, as famously recited in the Heart Sutra, a Mahayana text written around the first century, "Form is emptiness; emptiness is form." Accordingly, emptiness is not non-existence. In other words, this is a really tough concept to grasp. What pondering the meaning of emptiness is trying to get at is an understanding of dependent origination—no phenomena exist on their own, independent of anything else. This book is only a book because the act of your reading it makes it so. Aside from its digital editions, it consists of pulp from a tree and bears symbols and figures that you attribute language and meaning to. To someone else, this object might be a doorstop. It doesn't have meaning independent of something or someone else. It has value only based on its dependence on another phenomenon—in this case, either the reader or the door-stopper.

As for the remaining Tibetan Buddhist sects, the Sakya school, also established in the eleventh century, was founded by a scholar known as Drogmi, who studied at the famous Vikramashila University in today's Bihar, India, under such teachers as Naropa, a great scholar after whom today's Naropa University in Boulder, Colorado, is named. Vikramashila, one of the great tantric learning centers of Buddhism, was home at its peak to more than one thousand students and a hundred teachers. It flourished for some four centuries before it was destroyed sometime around the year 1200 by the armies of Bakhtiyar Khilji, an Islamic general of the Dehli Sultanate. Leadership of the Sakya school is hereditary, passing as it does from generation to generation within a particular family.

The Geluk school, which emphasizes monastic discipline, as well as a union of tantric practices and the study of Buddhist sutras, was founded in the fourteenth century by Je Tsongkhapa. Tsongkhapa was revered as a great scholar and, like Guru Rinpoche is referred to by his disciples as the "second Buddha." Unlike many other Buddhist figures before him, Tsongkhapa left eighteen volumes of his specific teachings, which are the foundation of Geluk practice today and protect against misinterpretation. The lineage of the Dalai Lamas, which was established in the seventeenth century, derives from the Geluk schools.

The Dalai Lama

The Dalai Lama, perhaps today's most newsworthy Buddhist with well over six million Twitter followers, was born Llamo Dhondup in 1935. The honorific title is loosely translated as "Ocean Teacher," indicating the depth of his wisdom. He is the fourteenth reigning Dalai Lama and considered both the spiritual leader of Tibet as well as, at one time, its exiled head of state. Tibetan Buddhism employs an ancient and mystical tradition of recognizing small children as the reincarnations of specific, past Buddhist masters. Accordingly, at the age of two, Llamo Dhondup was recognized by senior monastics as the reincarnation of the thirteenth Dalai Lama and given the name Tenzin Gyatso. As such, the Dalai Lama is considered by his followers to have been born as an already enlightened being who delayed his entry into nirvana in order to serve humanity.

Still, he had to go to school. After an intensive period of study, the Dalai Lama assumed his office and political power in 1950, when he was fifteen years old, one year after China's invasion of Tibet. He attempted throughout the 1950s to reach a political accommodation with the Chinese government but was unable to secure Tibetan independence from Chairman Mao Zedong. Finally, in 1959, with the brutal suppression of a Tibetan national uprising in the capital of Lhasa, and under a perceived threat of assassination, he, along with tens of thousands of his followers, was forced to flee the country. Since then, and until today, he has lived in Dharamsala in northern India. The Chinese government considers the Dalai Lama to be a separatist and a traitor, and has even criticized him as a terrorist who incites Tibetan rebellion.

In part, China's hard-line rhetoric toward the Dalai Lama wasn't helped by the discovery in 1998 of a CIA-backed effort throughout the 1960s, which was supported by the Dalai Lama, to train and arm Tibetan resistance fighters. The U.S. Central Intelligence Agency, as part of the country's containment policy against Communist regimes at the time, delivered some $1.7 million per year to the Tibetan Government in Exile, along with a $180,000-a-year stipend used by the Dalai Lama to set up offices in Geneva and New York and on international political lobbying. The Chinese government reportedly also resents the Dalai Lama's now-deep ties to India.

While serving as a head of state in exile, the Dalai Lama set forth a series of proposals meant to transfer power to an elected, representative government at the time that Tibet may one day regain its independence from China. Further, his "Five Point Peace Plan," which has been rejected by the Chinese government, calls for Tibet to become a "zone of peace," as well as a democratic and nuclear-free nation. In 2011, however, the Dalai Lama formally resigned as Tibet's head of state. China responded by calling his resignation "a trick."

Early political miscues aside, and with the CIA adventure long since ended, the Dalai Lama, together with a great number of courageous Tibetan

The Venerable Chogyam Trungpa Rinpoche, founder of Naropa University, at a gathering
on campus in the 1970s.

Buddhists, has maintained a position of nonviolence despite exile and brutal
authoritarian pressures. In recognition of his efforts, as well as the nonviolent
struggle of the Tibetan people, he received the Nobel Peace Prize in 1989. Over
the years, the Dalai Lama has travelled to more than sixty countries, written
approximately seventy books, spoken out to offer Buddhist perspectives on
subjects as diverse as the environment, vegetarianism, sexuality, and economics,
and has met with heads of state, prominent religious leaders, and numerous
other well-known individuals from a variety of fields.

Although the Dalai Lama is technically the leader of the Geluk school
of Tibetan Buddhism, he is universally respected by all Tibetan Buddhist
practitioners—particularly those in the West. Many American lay believers
have reported meeting him and being impressed by his charisma, humility,
kindness, and consideration. And while he continues to be held, for the most
part, in respect by virtually all Tibetan Buddhists, some Tibetan nationalists and
those seeking to resist the Chinese occupation have attempted, unsuccessfully,
to marginalize his political influence, believing that his comments in support
of nonviolence are increasingly ineffective.

The Dalai Lama also has been involved in a long-running controversy
with certain Sakya and Geluk practitioners, including Geshe Kalsang's New

Kadampa Tradition, who worship Dorje Shugden, a deity considered to be something of a guardian angel. The Dalai Lama banned the practice, out of concern that Dorje Shugden not be elevated to a level greater than the Buddha, which has resulted in numerous internal protests. Followers of Dorje Shugden in Dharamsala have also accused mainstream Tibetan Buddhist authorities of denying them access to hospitals and social services. Clashes between the two camps have occasionally been violent, and a prominent monk who supported the Dalai Lama's position was murdered in India under suspicious circumstances in 1997.

Yet another controversy in Tibet concerning the Dalai Lama pertains to his recognition of the seventeenth Karmapa, the individual chosen to lead the Kagyu school of Buddhism. There were two competing candidates, and the controversy caused a deep split in the Kagyu community. The Dalai Lama was criticized for even commenting on which Karmapa may be genuine: historically, as leader of the Geluk school, his opinion carries little authority. Moreover, oddly, the Dalai Lama's preferred candidate is also the one backed by the Chinese government.

Although the Dalai Lama, as popular as he is in the West, is the major figure responsible for the dissemination of Tibetan Buddhism to America, the true herald of Vajrayana practice, and the man most responsible for first turning the Tibetan dharma wheel in the United States, was the brilliant, mad, hard-living and wildly controversial Chogyam Trungpa Rinpoche.

Trungpa Rinpoche's Crazy Wisdom

Trungpa Rinpoche (the latter an honorific meaning "precious jewel") lived a fast, intense, and relatively short life, yet was considered a master in both the Kagyu and Nyingma traditions. He was an artist, a poet, a translator, and a teacher, and also the founder of Shambhala International, which now has more than a hundred meditation centers established all over America. His teachings are often summed up as having embodied "crazy wisdom." Trungpa Rinpoche was an iconoclast, and, in that pioneering sense, the perfect person to bring Vajrayana Buddhism to America.

He was born in rural Tibet in 1939. According to his own account, on the day of his birth a rainbow was seen in his village, a pail containing water was somehow found full of milk, and several of his extended family members dreamed that a lama visited their tents. At the age of twenty, in 1959, Trungpa Rinpoche led a group of his followers by horseback and foot out of the mountains of Tibet and into Dharamsala, on the heels of the fleeing Dalai Lama, in a grueling journey that lasted more than a year. There, he began to study English and eventually made his way to Oxford University in 1963. In 1967 he helped to establish the first Tibetan Buddhist monastery in the West, in Scotland, where he counted rock star David Bowie, among others, as a meditation student. Two years later, he suffered a near fatal accident when he crashed his car into a Scottish joke and humor shop.

The accident left him permanently paralyzed on the left side and was attributed to either lack of sleep or drunk driving. The near-death experience caused him to dramatically rethink his life, but he did not stop drinking; rather, he determined to give up his monastic vows and work as a lay teacher. And although he continued his extraordinary work as a teacher, with a particularly keen understanding of how to communicate the tenets of Vajrayana Buddhism to a Western audience, he also became notorious for indulging his passions for women, alcohol, and tobacco.

In 1970, Trungpa Rinpoche brought both his wealthy, sixteen-year-old, newly acquired English wife and Tibetan Buddhism to America. He established himself in Boulder, Colorado, the landscape of which reminded him of Tibet, and began to teach there at the University of Colorado. He was embraced quickly by his American disciples as a master of meditation. In 1974, Trungpa Rinpoche founded the Naropa Institute, now known as Naropa University, adjacent to the University of Colorado's campus. This first accredited Buddhist university in the United States immediately attracted some of America's best writers and creative artists, many from the Beat tradition, including Allen Ginsburg and Ann Waldman, as well as William Burroughs, Gregory Bateson, and John Cage. Ginsburg, in particular, became a devoted Trungpa Rinpoche disciple. He founded at Naropa the Jack Kerouac School for Disembodied Poetics, and the University's library today bears Ginsburg's name.

With the founder in residence in the mid-1970s, the Naropa campus, not unlike other schools of the era, was known for its party atmosphere. According to the celebrated yogi Bhagavan Das, in his memoir, *It's Here Now (Are You?)*, "that's basically what Naropa was: a huge blowout party, twenty-four hours a day—different parties all over town. It was school all day, party all night." But there were also present a majority of very dedicated Buddhist practitioners, including the writer Jack Kornfield and a future Naropa University president, the former Merce Cunningham dancer Barbara Dilley, pursuing a serious quest for enlightenment.

"Trungpa Rinpoche was many things," Dilley says. "He was both a constellation and a rascal. He came to the Western world from traditional Tibet with tremendous mind practices but without the English language. He was a meditative master and extremely brilliant. I think in some ways it was a lonely path."

Trungpa Rinpoche's path, as it were, was grounded in his Tibetan Vajrayana tradition but inspired by his vision of Shambhala—the magical, pure land of Tibetan Buddhist myth, said to be hidden somewhere in Central Asia. He defined it, however, not as a physical place but as the root of human goodness and aspiration. Shambhala, accordingly, was his dream of a renewed, revitalized civilization that, through sincere Buddhist practice by enough people, actually could be realized.

John Cobb, an attorney and also a past Naropa president, characterizes the university's founder in the context of the Dalai Lama: "The Dalai Lama is a man of overwhelming consideration. Trungpa Rinpoche, too, was tremendously kind and present. But he also had a vast social vision to create an enlightened society."

Trungpa Rinpoche's concept of a Buddhist "warrior," which appears often in his writings, is derived from his unique perspective on faith coupled with the primordial teachings, or the natural wisdom, of the Tibetan people as expressed in their traditional concepts of common sense as well as the cultural mores of the nativist Bon religion. Perhaps his greatest achievement was to introduce the esoteric Vajrayana practices—a secretive methodology traditionally reserved for monks in the monastery—to lay men and women in America.

Trungpa Rinpoche spoke and wrote often of synchronizing mind and body through the practice of meditation and developing the "sad and tender heart of the warrior." This sadness, according to him, doesn't come from mistreatment or even from the more traditional Buddhist concern about attaching oneself to external desires. Rather, it stems from having a naked, open heart completely exposed and sensitive to the sufferings of the world. It comes from training yourself, through meditation, to be who you are, from emptying your mind of impermanent thoughts and delusion to the extent that you're compelled to give yourself fully to others. This sadness, he held, is more of an enlightened condition, a result of seeing the world vividly, and it is the effect of mastering Trungpa Rinpoche's training. By the mid-1980s he had thousands of American disciples, a trail of lurid stories, and close to a hundred meditation centers established throughout the country.

But then he left the United States for Nova Scotia because, in Dilley's view, he "had concluded that his vision could not be realized in American society." He continued to drink heavily and ultimately passed away two years later, at the age of forty-eight, in Canada, from causes relating to diabetes, high blood pressure and a chronic abuse of alcohol. So who was this man: a self-indulging, hard-living Tibetan exile, or a supreme teacher to the West of profound and, until then, secret tantric Buddhist practices? Could he have been both?

Although a number of explicit controversies have been attached to Trungpa Rinpoche dating back to the 1970s, almost none of his contemporaneous practitioners, including the respected writer and Buddhist nun Pema Chodron, doubt his genius for teaching Buddhism. Still, several published criticisms of Trungpa Rinpoche's methods come close to calling the sangha that he nurtured a cult. John Steinbeck's son and his wife wrote a critical memoir of their former mentor in which they claimed, among other things, that Trungpa Rinpoche not only abused alcohol but also Seconal and cocaine. Another incident involved the poet W.S. Merwin, who had in 1975 attended an intensive training session with Trungpa Rinpoche without having previously been enrolled in the several years' worth of Vajrayana study required of other participants. After Merwin and his girlfriend refused to disrobe at a Halloween party during which many people, including, reportedly, Trungpa Rinpoche, danced in the nude, they were taken from their room and forcibly stripped while their pleas to call the police were ignored. Nevertheless, Merwin stayed for the remainder of the intensive session, though he later advised others not to become Trungpa Rinpoche's students.

How do these alleged events square with the otherwise selfless, traditional images of founding Buddhist personalities, including the Buddha himself or Kumarajiva? Is there something about Trungpa Rinpoche's crazy wisdom that is impossible for non-acolytes to grasp? Or is it just crazy?

Crazy wisdom, or holy madness, wasn't invented by Trungpa Rinpoche—it's a modality found in many tantric traditions, including Vajrayana, in which the mentor employs seemingly unspiritual tactics in order to awaken his disciple's seeking spirit. In Trungpa Rinpoche's own words:

> If a bodhisattva is completely selfless, a completely open person, then he will act according to openness, will not have to follow rules; he will simply fall into patterns. It is impossible for the bodhisattva to destroy or harm other people, because he embodies transcendental generosity. He has opened himself completely and so does not discriminate between this and that. He just acts in accordance with what is…. [H]is mind is so precise, so accurate that he never makes mistakes. He never runs into unexpected problems, never creates chaos in a destructive way.

In this context, then, compelling Merwin and his girlfriend to strip, may be seen as a crazy-wisdom, "skillful means" vehicle to shock Merwin into dropping his guard and awakening his Buddha nature. Are acts of crazy wisdom a test of the disciple's devotion? Similarly, Trungpa Rinpoche's journey into alcohol abuse may be viewed, generously, as his submission to the very depths of the problems affecting Americans so that he could understand them better and, presumably, lead others to rise above them.

In part, of course, the quite human aspect of Trungpa Rinpoche also must be understood in the context of the guru as an infallible and paramount figure in the Vajrayana tradition. There seems, perhaps, to have been a certain commitment to secrecy: a sort of what happens in Naropa, stays in Naropa. But this is not out of the ordinary for a Vajrayana master and his disciples. Vows of personal secrecy are common to Vajrayana gurus.

Shunryu Suzuki of the San Francisco Zen Center once defended Trungpa Rinpoche's actions as follows: "You may criticize him because he drinks alcohol like I drink water, but that is a minor problem. He trusts you completely. He knows that if he is always supporting you in a true sense you will not criticize him, whatever he does. And he doesn't mind whatever you say. That is not the point, you know. This kind of big spirit, without clinging to some special religion or form of practice, is necessary for human beings."

Nevertheless, given Trungpa Rinpoche's profound teachings, it appears at least from the perspective of contemporary Western values that Trungpa Rinpoche personally suffered a lot. It's true, of course, that suffering is one of the Four Noble Truths. But Buddhism is supposed to provide a road map to transform that suffering into enlightenment.

Was his alcoholism an aspect of his religious teaching, or was it the effect of having been torn away from his country by an authoritarian regime and made to live his life in a strange and hostile West? Or was it the response of his sad and tender heart to the perception of devastating suffering that Trungpa Rinpoche observed throughout his short but turbulent life? As Buddhism teaches, it is hard enough to understand our own minds—let alone the minds of others.

Responsibility for the Vajrayana and Shambhala traditions established in the United States by Trungpa Rinpoche have been assumed by his son, Sakyong Mipham Rinpoche. Among the other younger, contemporary teachers of Tibetan Buddhism in North America are Pema Chodron and Dzigar Kongtrul Rinpoche. Each of these individuals, as well as the contemporary administration of Naropa University, maintains a sober and serious approach to religion and academics, respectively. Accordingly, Trungpa Rinpoche's wisdom has been transmitted to this next generation: his craziness not so much.

4

The Lotus Position:
Nichiren, Daisaku Ikeda, and the Soka Gakkai

The sixth-century scholar Zhiyi was among the first Chinese Buddhist masters to elaborate a complete and systematic classification of all of the Buddha's teachings. As a result of his organizational work, he is credited, among other things, with asserting that the Lotus Sutra is supreme among them.

Zhiyi became a Buddhist monk following the sudden deaths of both of his parents and the subsequent military conquest of his hometown, Jiangling, when he was seventeen years old. He received much of his Buddhist training at monasteries near Mount T'ien-t'ai, close to the modern city of Taizhou. The name of this mountain ultimately became synonymous with Zhiyi and his centuries-long renown. Although Zhiyi was a contemporary of Bodhidharma, they apparently never met. And notably, Zhiyi, unlike Bodhidharma, throughout his career suffered little by way of official persecution, because he enjoyed the support of China's ruling classes at the time.

Among his important works, many of which constitute the philosophical basis of the Tendai and Nichiren schools of Buddhism, Zhiyi categorized Shakyamuni's teachings into five stages, the last of which, the Lotus and Nirvana Sutra stage, he considered to be the Buddha's essential teachings. He also set forth the concept of Three Thousand Realms in a Single Thought Moment, a notion that was critical to the philosophical perspective adopted by Nichiren seven hundred years later in Japan.

Zhiyi, through this concept of Three Thousand Realms, opened a window on the fleeting moment-by-moment nature of life, which, in turn, gives rise to the ideal that anyone—including men and, radically, women—has the capacity to transform suffering into enlightenment. His masterwork, known as *Great Concentration and Insight*, states:

> *Life at each moment is endowed with the Ten Worlds. At the same time, each of the Ten Worlds is endowed with all Ten Worlds, so that an entity of life actually possesses one hundred worlds. Each of these worlds in turn possesses thirty realms, which means that in the one hundred worlds there are three thousand realms. The three thousand realms of existence are all possessed by life in a single moment. If there is no life, that is the end of the matter. But if there is the slightest bit of life, it contains all the three thousand realms.... This is what we mean when we speak of the "region of the unfathomable."*

Zhiyi's views on the Lotus Sutra profoundly inspired Nichiren—considered by many Buddhist scholars to be one of the most divisive and misunderstood figures in the history of Buddhism. And Nichiren's thirteenth century Buddhist movement, in turn, ultimately led to the establishment of the Soka Gakkai in the United States some seven hundred years hence.

Nichiren was born in 1222 to a poor family of fishermen on the coast of Japan, in present-day Chiba Prefecture. He was ordained as a monk at the age of sixteen, at a temple called Seicho-ji, and then embarked on a long and exhaustive journey to study at all of the major Buddhist schools predominant at that time throughout Kamakura, Nara, and Kyoto. These efforts included his years-long study of the Tendai, Zen, Shingon, and Pure Land schools, the last of which encourages prayer to an entity known as Amida Buddha for salvation in the next life. In 1253, when he was thirty-two, Nichiren concluded that Zhiyi was correct: the Lotus Sutra was the highest and most profound teaching of the Buddha. Moreover, Nichiren determined that the essence of this teaching was to be found in two specific chapters of the sutra, as well as in its very title: *Myoho-Renge-Kyo*, or Mystic Law of the Lotus Sutra.

In the first of these critical chapters, the second chapter of the Lotus Sutra, Shakyamuni's words are recorded to reveal that the purpose of his advent is to lead all people to enlightenment. "All people" means everyone, irrespective of social standing, education, or gender. Specifically, Shakyamuni here declares that only Buddhas can realize the true aspect of all phenomena, which consist of ten particular factors of life. This revelation established the theoretical basis for Zhiyi's assertion of three thousand conditions of life in a single moment—and his corollary that all people, accordingly, have the potential to attain Buddhahood. Moreover, in this chapter, Shakyamuni states that his earlier teachings, or sutras, were merely expedient means meant to lead people to the one, not quite identified, true Buddha vehicle. In a sense, both Zhiyi and Nichiren perceived within this chapter a clarification by Shakyamuni that his sermons from the prior thirty years, many of which served throughout history as foundational elements for numerous Buddhist sects, were actually partial revelations of truth.

The second of the key chapters—the sixteenth chapter of the Lotus Sutra—reveals that Shakyamuni actually attained enlightenment not during his lifetime in India but over immeasurably countless eons ago. The intent of this teaching is meant to demonstrate, first, the incalculably long period during which life, in reality, exists. Second, and more profoundly, it illustrates Shakyamuni's enlightened view that he has, over eternity, not passed into a state of nirvana, or freedom from suffering, but has rather returned again and again in different forms to help ordinary people aspire to enlightenment. Nichiren, following his years of study and meditation, grasped the expression of this unprecedented, universal law as revealed by Shakyamuni—what Buddhism later described as "nonregression"—to be precisely the law of *Nam-myoho-renge-kyo*. The action of chanting this expression, in Nichiren's revolutionary view, is itself the "one true Buddha vehicle." According to Nichiren, this law transcends Shakyamuni's earlier teachings, which prescribed a virtually superhuman task of achieving enlightenment through fifty-two stages of bodhisattva practice, because it allows a practitioner who chants *Nam myoho renge-kyo* to cut immediately to the heart of Buddhist enlightenment.

The Life of Nichiren

In April 1253, Nichiren returned to Seicho-ji, then a Tendai temple, and proclaimed that the chanting of *Nam-myoho-renge-kyo*—literally, Devotion To the Mystic Law of the Lotus Sutra—and the recitation of these essential chapters of the Lotus Sutra, was the correct practice for his time and beyond. He was denounced and chased off of the temple grounds.

Far from seeking accommodation, though, Nichiren began to propagate his teachings throughout Kamakura, then the capital of Japan, and he wrote numerous essays and treatises that directly confronted the major Buddhist schools of the time, primarily Zen, Shingon, Pure Land, and Tendai. These writings, known as Gosho, hundreds of which still survive today, are unique in that they relate Nichiren's experiences, in his own hand, in a form that's literate, accessible, and fortified by logical reasoning. The letters offer an unusual window into the character of an ancient, flesh-and-blood Buddhist teacher—many are written to women, who were, in Nichiren's cutting edge view, as capable of attaining enlightenment as men. Still others are even written to children. Although Nichiren is notorious for his fiery rhetoric against the Japanese Buddhist sects prevalent in his day, his many letters also express tender and poignant emotions toward the recipients and their mundane problems. More than anything, though, Nichiren's Gosho sets forth with passion, and in a confrontational, uncompromising attitude, why he believed that the Lotus Sutra was supreme. He relies in great measure on the earlier writings of Zhiyi, as well as those of Zhiyi's disciples Miao-lo and Dengyo—the Japanese monk, also known to history as Saicho, who traveled to China in the ninth century and first established the Tendai sect in Japan.

Nichiren was what today we might call "in your face." He criticized Zen for what he called great arrogance, disparaging claims by its practitioners to be equal to the Buddha. He suggested, publicly, that Zen could not possibly transmit something apart from Buddhist teachings, because apart from the teachings there could be no principles. He argued that "talk about the twirled flower, the faint smile, and something being entrusted to Mahakasyapa" is itself a teaching, as is the notion of a Buddhist philosophy independent of words or writing. The bedrock Zen principle equating the mind to the Buddha, and the Buddha to the mind, was, for Nichiren, a partial truth that led people astray.

These are strong words. But he reserved even greater criticism for the Pure Land sect, also referred to as Nembutsu, which was founded by Honen. Nichiren went so far as to suggest that Nembutsu, a "devilish teaching," ought to be outlawed. In his view, the Nembutsu practice, which concerns salvation in a "pure land" sometime after death, was such a transgression from Shakyamuni's teachings that benevolent deities who once protected Japan would no longer appear and that Buddhism, itself, was threatened with ruin.

Japan at this time was subject to numerous natural disasters, including earthquakes, astronomical disturbances, terrible storms, and famine. People were starving and dying, and warlords feuded for control of the nation. Many historians note that this period, due to such acute stresses in Japanese society, was ripe for religious reformation. Kamakura, in particular, was controlled at this time by shoguns who had embraced the Nembutsu teachings. Nichiren, never one to mince words or compromise in any way, and who had gone so far as to predict a foreign invasion of the country due to its embrace of what he considered to be incorrect teachings, incited an onslaught of persecution against himself.

Nichiren's analysis of the Lotus Sutra, as well as the Nirvana, Diamond, and many other sutras, was particularly provocative, because he insisted that of all the words of the Buddha, only the Lotus Sutra promised enlightenment to each individual, without regard to economic, gender, or social status. This is a message that leaders of the other Buddhist schools, privileged as they were by their government patrons, did not care to consider. This political-religious status quo at the time, coupled with Nichiren's vociferous and inflexible stance, resulted in his two exiles and two further attempts on his life.

In 1260, Nichiren published a treatise known as the *Rissho Ankoku Ron*, or On Establishing the Correct Teaching For the Peace of the Land, which predicted a specific invasion of Japan by the Mongol Empire should the country's rulers not come to their senses and embrace his true Buddhism. In response, the government exiled him, dropping him on a slick rock, at low tide, in the middle of the Pacific Ocean off of the then-remote Izu Peninsula. He was serendipitously saved by a passing fisherman and returned to Kamakura two years later.

In 1271 Nichiren was abducted from a hut in which he lived near Kamakura and taken by soldiers led by Hei no Saemon, the deputy chief of the Hojo Regency's Office of Military and Police Affairs, who was ordered by the Regent to seize the monk. What happened next is as close as it gets to a Buddhist thriller.

According to Nichiren's detailed recollection of events, Hei no Saemon arrived in the middle of the night with several hundred armored warriors. After speaking to Nichiren in a rough and threatening manner, Hei no Saemon's chief retainer assaults the monk, snatches a volume of the Lotus Sutra from inside of his robes, and strikes him in the face with it three times. The retainer then throws the scroll on the floor of the hut, and several of the other warriors ransack the place and trample on and destroy nine other Lotus Sutra scrolls.

They apprehended Nichiren and paraded him down a street toward the execution grounds known as Tatsunokuchi, all of which today is part of urban Kamakura. At one point, while passing a shrine dedicated to a Buddhist deity known as Hachiman, Nichiren asked the procession to pause. He dismounted, approached the shrine, and made the following appeal to the deity:

> *If I am executed tonight and go to the pure land of Eagle Peak, I will dare to report to Shakyamuni Buddha, the lord of teachings, that the Sun Goddess and Great Bodhisattva Hachiman are the deities who have broken their oath to him. If you feel this will go hard with you, you had better do something about it right away!*

He then remounted his horse, and the warriors, with Nichiren and four of his samurai-disciples now in tow, arrived at the execution grounds. What happened next is what Nichiren in certain of his writings refers to as the death of the common mortal Nichiren and the birth of the true votary of the Lotus Sutra.

The party reached the execution grounds sometime before dawn, yet still in the black of early-hours night. The soldiers grew excited, milling around Nichiren in anticipation of what was to be his decapitation. By now, several of Nichiren's samurai-disciples had joined him with tears in their eyes, lamenting his last moments. As the time for the fateful deed approached, and in the midst of Nichiren's offering of some final words to one of his closest disciples, an atmospheric disturbance, described by Nichiren as "a brilliant orb as bright as the moon," streaked across the sky, illuminating both the ground and the faces of the soldiers. In the thirteenth century, perhaps not even any more so than today, such an occurrence—apparently either an extraordinarily well-timed comet or a very large meteorite—was interpreted by those present as a divine intervention. According to Nichiren, the executioner "fell on his face," and the soldiers, in a panic, began to disperse. Nichiren, in an act of defiance reserved for those only of supreme confidence and unflinching mission, called out for them to return and begged them to finish the job before dawn.

But the warriors, fearful of Nichiren's apparently miraculous powers, refused to carry on with the deed. Rather, they took him to the home of a top police official, where Nichiren continued to denounce Zen, Pure Land, and the other Buddhist schools and asserted the supremacy of the Lotus Sutra. Within a month, however, the Regent decided that Nichiren was to be sent far away, to Sado Island, a hostile and foreboding environment in the western Sea of Japan, from which he was not expected to return. He survived the journey over mountains and the sea and found shelter in the middle of a cemetery:

> *In the yard around the hut the snow piled deeper and deeper. No one came to see me; my only visitor was the piercing wind. Great Concentration and Insight and the Lotus Sutra lay open before my eyes, and Nam-myoho-renge-kyo flowed from my lips. My evenings passed in discourse to the moon and stars on the fallacies of the various schools and the profound meaning of the Lotus Sutra. Thus, one year gave way to the next.*

He was exiled to Sado for three years and released only after the Mongols indeed did attempt to invade Japan, in 1274, as Nichiren had warned. Thereafter, recognizing that the Regent would not embrace his teachings, he retired to a mountain retreat, where he wrote many letters to his disciples and also inscribed a mandala known as the Dai-Gohonzon, meant to be the object of worship for his followers.

As is often the manner throughout the history of Buddhism, Nichiren's disciples disagreed with each other and split into several different schools soon after the master's death in 1282. Among these schools was Nichiren Shoshu, which, led by Nichiren's closest disciple Nikko Shonin, held the Dai-Gohonzon, and established a temple at the foot of Mount Fuji. For close to 700 years, the monks of this obscure sect passed down Nichiren's teachings, but they remained small and virtually unknown outside of Japan until they encountered a man called Tsunesaburo Makiguchi, a Japanese schoolteacher, in the early twentieth century.

The Founding of the Soka Gakkai and Its Demise During World War II

Makiguchi and his younger, close associate, Josei Toda, converted to Nichiren Shoshu in 1928. Both of these educators sought to reform the Japanese public educational system and, inspired in part by Western "humanistic" educators from Montaigne through John Dewey, they published works and agitated for reforms that would minimize the pedagogical method of rote memorization prevalent in the school system at the time and develop a more student-centered approach to classroom education. Specifically, Makiguchi was against the concept of education serving the State, as expressed as official policy in Japan's Imperial Rescript on Education, and rather believed that the purpose of education was to advance the happiness of each individual student. Makiguchi and Toda found in the humanistic, anti-authoritarian teachings of Nichiren a deep philosophical source that would underscore their educational objectives.

In 1930, Makiguchi and Toda established the forerunner of today's Soka Gakkai—the Society for the Creation of Value. Intended at first to be purely a gathering of teachers, the organization throughout the 1930s grew to include several hundred educators, most of whom converted to Nichiren Buddhism but with the express intent to implement the teaching ideals that Makiguchi espoused.

Meanwhile, the Japanese war machine advanced. From 1937 to 1938, Japan invaded China, the Soviet Union, and Mongolia. And in December 1941, Japan drew the United States into World War II after the bombing of Pearl Harbor in Hawaii.

For the better part of the previous seventy years, Japan had created a cult of emperor worship under the guise of State Shinto. In particular, during World War II, the Japanese government, for the sake of national unity, sought to consolidate all religious groups under this State Shinto banner. Accordingly, all temples and religious organizations in Japan were compelled to accept a State Shinto talisman, which would imply the subservience of the respective religious order under the authority of the emperor and State Shinto. All Zen temples, as well as Nichiren Shoshu, complied. The Soka Gakkai, as an affiliated lay organization of Nichiren Shoshu, was ordered to likewise accept the talisman. But Makiguchi and Toda, asserting the primacy of Nichiren's teachings, resisted, as did a few other individuals with ties to both Christian and Communist groups.

Whereas Nichiren Shoshu went so far as to provide timber from its head temple grounds for use by the Japanese military, Makiguchi and Toda, for their part, were arrested in 1943 as enemies of the state. The Soka Gakkai was disbanded.

Tsunesaburo Makiguchi (seated) and
Josei Toda, the founders of the Soka
Gakkai. Both were imprisoned in
Japan during World War II.

Makiguchi, then seventy-two years old, throughout his incarceration refused to acknowledge the supremacy of the Emperor and withheld support for the Japanese war effort. He died in prison in 1944, prior to the end of the war, from causes resulting from malnutrition.

Upon learning of his mentor's death, Toda, then in his mid-forties, vowed, perhaps in part as an act of revenge, to rebuild the Soka Gakkai upon the end of the war. He also later expressed his belief that he had attained a profound understanding of the nature of life—essentially, enlightenment—as a result of his continuous study of the Lotus Sutra and his assiduous chanting of *Nam-myoho-renge-kyo* while imprisoned. Upon his release from jail in July 1945, just prior to the nuclear attacks on Hiroshima and Nagasaki, Toda immediately set to work on his goal. The Soka Gakkai was reestablished not as a teacher's organization but as a religious laypersons movement affiliated with Nichiren Shoshu that was now intended to serve all of humankind.

Daisaku Ikeda and the SGI in America

In 1947 Toda met a nineteen-year-old man named Daisaku Ikeda, who had lost an elder brother and his family's home in the war and would become Toda's closest disciple. Toda took it upon himself to personally nurture Ikeda in a broad range of fields, a process that the younger man often characterized as a university-level education. In turn, Ikeda decided to forestall his college education in order to study directly with Toda, and to help his mentor rebuild his struggling businesses and establish the Soka Gakkai as a modern, post-war Japanese religious movement. All of what Ikeda later accomplished, he has repeatedly said, has its source in his relationship with Toda, his mentor. This includes the eventual founding, by Ikeda, of various institutions that include

Soka University, Soka University of America, the Tokyo Fuji Art Museum, the Min-On Concert Association, and the Toda Institute for Global Peace and Policy Studies, among many others.

Together, Toda and Ikeda, in a remarkable and intense religious struggle, rebuilt their Buddhist movement into an expanded force that by Toda's death in 1958—a period of eleven years—had reached an active and devoted membership of more than 800,000 families in Japan. Thereafter, Ikeda, at thirty-two, became Soka Gakkai president in 1960 and launched its worldwide presence with his first overseas trip that year to the United States.

Other Nichiren-related temples had been established in America as early as 1904, but they failed to gain a following outside of the Japanese immigrant population and later were disbanded as part of the U.S. government's policy against Japanese-Americans during the war. In comparison, the Soka Gakkai, at first known as NSA, or Nichiren Shoshu of America, and now known as Soka Gakkai International-USA, or SGI-USA, quickly attracted a large and diverse following that extended far outside of parochial Japanese immigrant communities.

The key to understanding Daisaku Ikeda and his Buddhist vision for happiness and peace is to be found in his relationship with Josei Toda. Similarly, the mentor-disciple relationship, with a contemporaneous focus on Ikeda as mentor, is paramount to practitioners in today's SGI-USA. It is the keystone of the SGI's ethos, character, diversity, and its successful propagation efforts. But, as a Buddhist association in the tradition of Nichiren, it should come as no surprise that the Soka Gakkai's development has been accompanied by considerable controversy and attack.

Like Nichiren, and so many of their Buddhist forebears going back as far as Shakyamuni, Ikeda has faced, quite literally on a daily basis, a torrent of criticism. In Japan, he's been accused, at various times, of being both a Communist and a fascist; he was briefly imprisoned on charges of political vote-buying, which were later proven in court to be false; and he's been portrayed by the media as a cult leader, a womanizer, or simply an egomaniac.

A *Los Angeles Times* piece published in 1996 gives a more balanced view of the man and his mission. The reporter acknowledged a frenzied anti-Ikeda industry in Japan but portrayed him as a soft-spoken and straightforward subject who, praised by such unassailable figures as Rosa Parks, Nelson

Mandela, and a rabbi of the Simon Wiesenthal Center's Museum of Tolerance, grew animated when denouncing the "demonic nature" of authority.

This so-called anti-Ikeda industry, which has certainly affected the image of the SGI in the United States, stems from three main sources: the fact that the organization, in the relatively distant past, aggressively proselytized; that the Soka Gakkai in Japan maintains a well-documented involvement in rough-and-tumble national politics; and that its permanent 1991 split from the Nichiren Shoshu clergy was very public and bitter. This split, among other effects, provided the Soka Gakkai with an extraordinarily unique position in the Buddhist world—that of a "protestant" Buddhist movement.

In November 1990, Ikeda invited a chorus assembled for a regular monthly meeting of Soka Gakkai representatives to sing "Ode To Joy," the Friedrich Schiller poem that Beethoven had set to music in the final movement of his Ninth Symphony. Following the performance, Ikeda publicly commented that people, including members of the Soka Gakkai, were free to sing any songs that they like and that Buddhism may be presented publicly through a variety of different means. He then encouraged the chorus to perform it once again.

Soon after, the high priest of Nichiren Shoshu, who was not present at the meeting, denounced the performance and Ikeda's comments as praising a non-Buddhist, Christian teaching. This was followed by a letter delivered to the Soka Gakkai leadership along with thirty-five demands, phrased as questions, designed to either cause the lay organization to submit to the high priest's authority—or cause it, and its seventeen million members worldwide, to be excommunicated.

Relations between the monastics and the Soka Gakkai were never great, dating back, of course, to Makiguchi's death and Toda's imprisonment in the 1940s. In fact, in 1979, the temple succeeded in having Ikeda resign, temporarily, as the Soka Gakkai leader. At the heart of the religious conflict was the assertion, by Nichiren Shoshu, that no Buddhist could achieve enlightenment without the intercession of a priest. Ikeda and the Soka Gakkai denied any such intermediating authority. As a result, in 1991, Nichiren Shoshu excommunicated all of the Soka Gakkai members, leaving it either free or adrift—depending on one's point of view—as the only significant Buddhist movement in history without an attendant clergy.

From an historical perspective, this episode, while unusual, isn't unprecedented. Bodhidharma, for one, preached the teachings of Zen in response to what he perceived to be the decline of true Buddhist practice in China. Miao-lo, the successor to Zhiyi six generations later, reformed the Chinese T'ient'ai school in response to the corruption of the original master's teachings. And of course Nichiren's entire career was an attempt to reawaken the teachings of Shakyamuni's Lotus Sutra in thirteenth century Japan. If anything, the matter of the clerical split appears to have not only energized Ikeda and his organization but has also freed them to shed some of the more arcane rituals and zealous emphases on propagation upon which the clergy had always insisted.

Ikeda's primary teaching is that the purpose of Buddhist practice is to achieve human revolution, a process of self-actualization that might be considered somewhat similar to the Buddha's emphasis on following the Eightfold Path. Ikeda believes, like other Buddhists, that happiness can only come from within, and that it is a delusion to think that a change in external circumstances will permanently affect one's internal sufferings. Moreover, the process of human revolution is dependent upon prayer, profound self-reflection, and self-awareness, and catalyzed by helping others in need. In Ikeda's view, the chanting of *Nam-myoho-renge-kyo* gives a practitioner the courage, energy, and muster to change oneself for the better. And if one person changes, others will follow, because—here comes dependent origination again—an internal transformation will necessarily manifest external effects. In Ikeda's view, if enough individuals transform themselves in such a way, then world peace becomes a reality. It's a classical Buddhist approach to social good that, somewhat like Trungpa Rinpoche's visions of Shambhala, has little to do with political or social theories and everything to do with personal transformation and individual enlightenment.

Ikeda has promulgated this view through a bestselling, multi-volume historical novel, *The Human Revolution*, as well as through many, many public lectures, writings, poems, dialogues with world figures, overseas trips to the United States and some fifty other countries, speeches to students at universities like Harvard and Columbia, and annual peace proposals submitted to the United Nations. He is the recipient of numerous awards that include hundreds of university honorary doctorates and professorships, high honors from heads of state, and peace awards from noted humanitarian organizations worldwide. But despite these recognitions, like many other of the pioneering figures who planted a deep root of Buddhism in the United States, he at times appears to be a paradox, or perhaps a mirror, upon which an observer might reflect whatever it is they think they want to see.

Who, then, is Daisaku Ikeda, the person? The thousands, if not millions, of Buddhists around the world who consider him their mentor have very intimate and specific views. The SGI-USA's weekly newspaper, the *World Tribune*, often features columns and commentaries from members of the organization about their experiences with Mr. Ikeda. Many write of how friendly and natural he is, and especially about how they were overwhelmed by his consideration or expressions of gratitude. The three following anecdotes might shed some light on who he is or, at the very least, how Soka Gakkai Buddhists tend to interact with him. The first is from a City University of New York graduate student in education:

> *My relationship with President Ikeda is very simple. To the exact degree that I have made the effort to put his teachings into practice, I have advanced in my life toward happiness. When I first started practicing decades ago, the mentor relationship didn't seem that central and I mostly focused on my own chanting. But I now see how important it is to have someone who has gone ahead of you and can point the way. In non-Buddhist matters too, for example after the 9/11 attacks, I felt really disoriented, not knowing how to understand what had happened. When I read his words about quenching the flames of hatred with a flood of dialogue, I could see the way forward. That's the kind of mentor he is to me.*

Another SGI-USA member, who works at the United Nations, elaborates on Daisaku Ikeda as mentor:

> *I would simply say President Ikeda is my mentor because he embodies the teachings of true Buddhism to the letter and character. Of course there are struggles but my fundamental faith in the mentor-disciple relationship and in President Ikeda in particular gives me a solid and unbreakable sense of security—one that is genuine and proven. Rather than lose my*

identity in some paternalistic figure, I learn new things about myself, life
and my relationship with the world, including my duty and ability to help
others. I have no patience for people who fall prey to unscrupulous egotists
who use others to prop up their own sense of worth, and I am absolutely
confident that my relationship with President Ikeda is the polar opposite
of this parasitic engagement. To the contrary, I feel as though President
Ikeda supports me beyond any proportion by which I might reply; for
example, he has given his life to finding ways to encourage people like
me, has personally given me gifts and messages on more occasions than I
can count, and thinks considerately of me despite the fact that there is one
mentor—him—and millions of believers, among which I am counted.

Finally, a third individual, who mentioned to Mr. Ikeda toward the end of a year that he was happy because he had lived that past year with more courage than he had ever lived before, recalls that the SGI president pounded a table three times and said: "Yes, yes, yes! Happiness equals courage. Happiness equals courage. Happiness equals courage!"

At the end of the *Los Angeles Times* profile, Ikeda himself reflects on both his life and the very purpose of Buddhism and states that the message is more important than the man: "The choice is between being a slave of authority or of holding to your beliefs, living for your convictions. This is the history of Buddhism for the past 3,000 years."

PART TWO

·

THE SECOND JEWEL:
THE DHARMA

·

5

Flower Power:
The Special Transmission of Zen

The second of Buddhism's Three Jewels is the dharma. The meaning of dharma differs among religions: Hindus, for example, define dharma as righteousness, or one's place in the cosmic universe. Buddhists generally consider the dharma to indicate the collection of the Buddha's teachings. In these next several chapters, it refers to the specific practices of each Buddhist school.

According to some sutras, dharma is considered to be the spiritual or mental sense that each person possesses. Just as the ears have hearing, and the eyes sight, dharma can be thought of as the sense that attaches to one's mind. Dharma is infinite and indestructible, a universal truth that spans both the material and spiritual realms. To practice the particular teachings of a Buddhist school is to practice its dharma.

Dharma, of course, is not to be confused with karma, although the practice of dharma may help to change one's karma! Karma is the collection of a person's causes, thoughts, words and actions. The practice of a correct dharma, therefore, will create new, positive causes and enable someone to change the predominant negative causes in his or her life.

Simply put, the dharma of Zen is the practice of learning to wake up. It is to see one's self. There's no institutionalized code of ethical conduct, no supreme being to worship, no one master to follow—not even the Buddha, and no one sutra to study or realize. Zen practice seeks the immutable truth, or Buddhahood, inherent in each person's life. It's up to the practitioner to discover it.

Zen is not about stress reduction, anger management, motorcycle maintenance, vegetarian cuisine, or golf. Although writers and speakers representing a lot of different disciplines claim to be "Zen" or "Zen-like," what they mean is that a single-minded devotion to purpose leads to a mastering of their particular field. It does not mean that they're enlightened—there is no Buddhist approach to golf putting or even gardening for that matter. As beautiful as Zen rock gardens may be, the practice at its heart seeks to master life itself. It's a method for training one's mind to be still and to remain in the present moment. And this is very difficult to accomplish.

Although the founding and development of Zen is attributed to Bodhidharma, in the sixth century, in China, its origin is said to be traced to the so-called Flower Sermon by Shakyamuni. According to the sermon, the compilation of which is believed by several scholars to have been written by ancient Zen masters around the time of the founding of the school, Shakyamuni one day appeared ready to preach to his disciples but instead said absolutely nothing. Rather, he handed a white lotus flower he was holding to his closest disciple, Mahakasyapa, who then smiled. It is said that through this act Shakyamuni transmitted the wisdom of his teachings to Mahakasyapa without words. The Flower Sermon attributes the following to Shakyamuni:

> *I possess the true Dharma eye, the marvelous mind of Nirvana, the true form of the formless, the subtle Dharma Gate that does not rest on words or letters but is a special transmission outside of the scriptures. This I entrust to Mahakasyapa.*

Such a statement, of course, is radical in the world of Buddhism—did Shakyamuni conspicuously state that he made a special transmission of his Buddhist wisdom outside of his close to fifty years of teachings? Whether or not this was actually uttered by the Buddha, or whether the event even took place, is probably irrelevant in any case. For one thing, Zen practitioners for centuries have indeed recited various scriptures and sutras as a part of their daily practices, and they continue to do so today in the United States. But more to the point, the authenticity of the Flower Sermon ought to matter little to Zen because it's clear that the school itself developed as a form of Buddhism that from its start rejected the sutras or doctrines and emphasized direct experience. After all, as D.T. Suzuki held, the actual practice of Zen is its essence, and any writings about it are no more than mere scaffolding. So what is this direct experience that Zen points toward?

Zen is to see your mind. Zen's object is to allow the student to acquire a new perspective to view life and all of its phenomena. It is to be utterly present in the present moment, to not walk like a zombie through your life and squander the precious opportunities each of us has to experience its wonders. Zen is to be filled with awe at life and to be free. D.T. Suzuki refers to the acquisition of such a viewpoint as a dramatic insight, after years of practice, which is so sudden and even illogical that he calls it a "mental catastrophe." Once you reach such freedom, according to Zen, you will instinctively be filled with consideration for others because compassion will naturally flow from you, and you'll want to help others by pointing them to the Buddha already within them.

Some seek to practice Zen because they want to be better people, others because they want a way to make better decisions or to have healthy relationships with family and friends. Zen is to go inside yourself to find the truth, which is already there. It may be said, from a Zen perspective, that the Buddha never actually preached the truth. Rather, he pointed to it: he suggested that it is there within each of us. In a sense, Zen believes that each person is his or her own monastery.

This reality of Zen, especially in the United States where there is little tradition or established standards of practice, is evident in the fact that Zen training differs considerably throughout the country from monastery to monastery. Moreover, many traditional distinctions between lay practitioners and monks, or even men and women, have dissolved.

Zen is surely about discipline, and the founding of the practice goes hand in hand with an ethos of hard work. One Zen master in the eighth century had a famous maxim: "One day without work, one day without food." Zen teaches that enlightenment can be found in the most mundane of work activities—in the preparation of food; the caretaking of gardens; the arrangement of flowers, rocks, and stones; and in the execution of a simple work of brush painting in black ink.

Zazen: The Key to Zen

The primary entry to Zen is meditation, and the form of meditation Zen Buddhists practice is *zazen*. Zazen is a study of one's own mind. It is the heart of Zen practice. It's an experiential practice: you have to do it in order to understand it. When a person engages in zazen and penetrates past his or her ephemeral thoughts and learns to quiet his or her mind, one finds the original stillness of mind, which is often described by practitioners as a clear, placid lake.

The place where you practice zazen is known as the *zendo*. A zendo can include a large room in a monastery, a smaller space at a neighborhood group meeting, or a quiet place in your home. Lay practitioner Zen Buddhists typically will practice zazen at home with occasional visits for dokusan, or guidance, and encouragement to monasteries or smaller neighborhood temples or Zen centers. It's important, of course, to create the perfect space in which to practice zazen at home. That place ought to be as quiet as possible, and, unless one has an empty room to spare, it would be helpful to select an area with a blank wall.

As do all Buddhist practitioners, Zen students will also want to create an altar in this space. There's no requirement for what has to go on the altar, but generally Zen Buddhists will arrange leaves or flowers, incense, a candle, and a small bowl or cup filled with water around a statue of the Buddha. These represent the elements of earth, air, fire, and water. One is not worshipping the Buddha or the statue, of course—rather, the practitioner is engaged in zazen, and the image of the Buddha is meant to remind him or her of one's enlightened self.

Newer Zen students will want to try to meditate, at first, for five to ten minutes, and then gradually increase the ability to sit quietly in zazen for up to forty-five minutes.

The objective for a beginner in zazen is to remain still, forget the past, drop any thought of the future, and experience the present moment. This is sometimes referred to as present moment awareness. Clothing should be loose. Most practitioners sit on the floor, on a small meditation cushion called a *zafu*. Legs are either folded or in a lotus position (although it's also fine in the beginning to sit on a chair). The back is straight. Breathing is deep and relaxed, and it's directed into the belly. One's mouth should be closed, and breathing is through the nose. The tongue should rest behind the front upper teeth, and eyes are partly opened, partly closed, gazing down perhaps three feet in front but not at anything in particular. Hands are in what is called the *mudra* position. In this arrangement, the dominant hand is palm up holding the other hand, which is also palm up. The thumbs just barely touch each other.

Once in this position, begin to count breaths. One of the best ways to do this, for beginners, is to count each breath up to ten, and then to count down for the next ten, repeating the process. As stray thoughts enter the mind, simply try to release them. One will find, of course, that the mind has a tough time shutting up, but try to stay in the present moment and not think about what's for lunch or the many other things planned for that day. It's okay to listen to sounds, like the singing of birds, but don't think about how pretty it sounds. Just focus on being mindful in the present moment.

Attention is centered inside the body in a place known as the *hara*, or, for those who practice Tai Chi, the *tan t'ien*. This area, generally a couple of inches below the navel, is considered the font of life force.

It's exceedingly difficult, at first, to stay in the present moment. Even if you're meditating at home, for example, and your home is incredibly quiet, you may be facing a wall, deep in your breathing exercises until your cat decides to rub against your leg. (For some reason, cats in particular are very attracted

A group of Zen practitioners engaged in zazen at Zen Mountain Monastery.

© Zen Mountain Monastery Archive.

to Buddhists either meditating or chanting—now, see how easy it is to get distracted?) Inevitably, the mind will acknowledge the cat, and then a series of thoughts will cascade: She needs to be let out, she's almost out of food, the closest pet shop is more expensive than the one several blocks away, which is next to the pizza place that has great Sicilian slices, . . . etc. So when this happens, acknowledge that the mind has lost its focus, and return back to the present and one's breath.

This practice trains one's mind to concentrate on the present moment. And this concentration, according to Zen, will stay with the practitioner as he or she proceeds through the rest of the day. Ultimately, a successful practice of zazen should lead not only to bliss and a taste of enlightenment, but also to the wakefulness throughout the day that comes from learning to focus on the present moment. In this way, when the cat rubs against your knee you feel the cat but nothing more. You're anchored in the present moment, as well as the next one, and the one after that. You don't think of what has to come next, or what the goal is for the day, or any planned tasks. Rather, one learns to experience the beauty that comes with mindfulness and living in the present.

All of the above postures are meant to promote the most relaxed position in which to meditate. But to sit still like this for a long period of time, perhaps for forty-five minutes, can be torturous at first. Inevitably one's legs or butt will start to become numb and fall asleep. Old joints that may be weak become extremely painful. There may be a tendency to want to slouch or shift position. But the objective is to be utterly still. In the old days, at traditional monasteries in Japan, a senior monk or master would rap someone fidgeting with a stick, called a *kyosaku*, if he were moving around too much. But today, in America, that senior monk will more than likely just bring over a chair.

Sitting still in a zendo, or a meditation room in a monastery, is surprisingly hard work. The beautiful, peaceful setting, tinkling bells, rhythmic liturgies, and burning incense all tend to support one's journey of contemplation. But if a person is overweight or otherwise ill, or if there are problems with one's back, knees, or ankles, the practice of zazen can be truly painful. Legs will shake and sometimes hurt so much that people start to grimace and sweat. Perhaps, as a student becomes serious about walking the Zen way, he or she will also grow much more aware of one's body and be motivated to lose weight and improve health in order to more effectively practice zazen. It is, especially at first, a physically demanding practice.

Why is this so? Zen is meant to be a method to train the mind to remain in the present moment. Doing so requires discipline. Only by learning to keep the body still can the mind also begin to achieve stillness. There is no shortcut. There's no book one might read to reach *satori*, the term in Zen for an enlightened perspective on life. Either engage the demanding practice head-on, or don't.

The Ten Stages of Zen

There are ten stages of practice in Zen. The first is known as "seeking the ox." The ox represents the true self, and the seeking out, or search, for the true self is considered the first step toward achieving an enlightened mind.

The second stage is known as "discovering the footprints." In this more advanced stage the practitioner continues to focus his or her mind and train in the art of present moment awareness. It's a stage of practice in which a person typically deepens his or her faith—along with both doubt and determination. The changes, still, are subtle. A student in this second stage of practice will also begin to contemplate a Zen koan. These seemingly illogical and unanswerable questions—such as, famously, what is the sound of one hand clapping?—are meant to smash through the logical mind of reasoning by which virtually all of us in society operate. These koans are typically anecdotes of some long-ago Zen master or statements or questions. Such statements, of course, along with the volumes of work meant to explain them, appear to run counter to Zen's assertion that it needs no teaching or sutra to achieve its goal. Nevertheless, there are no inherent truths meant to be communicated by the koan; rather, it's a device used to point the Zen practitioner toward his or her own enlightened mind. In other words, there's really no right answer to the question posed.

Stage three of Zen Buddhist practice is called "first glimpse of the ox." It occurs in a deep state of meditation, when, for the briefest flash, the self and all of its senses are forgotten. This flash of enlightenment, if that is what it is, is typically accompanied by a notion that all external phenomena have fallen away. Some have described it as a state of brilliance, accompanied by a feeling of one's life being solitary yet permeating the universe. It's sometimes said that this flash, or glimpse of the ox, is potentially a dangerous juncture in one's quest for enlightenment. Interestingly, the glimpse of the ox is literally that—practitioners experiencing this state actually perceive a large, four-legged animal. Moreover, many people come to believe after this experience that they've grasped enlightenment, when they really haven't. There are seven more stages to go. This third stage of practice might last for years, depending on the student's devotion and zazen abilities, and it includes the contemplation of many more koans.

The fourth stage is called "catching the ox." Here, the ox is meant to represent the ego. It is at this stage that the practitioner begins to master the art of mindfulness. The ability to reach a deep meditative state and to focus on the present moment starts to manifest in every act that the Zen student takes—whether walking, eating, or even having sex.

The fifth stage of Zen practice is known as "taming the ox." As the ability to become mindful is enhanced, the ox—or the ego—is increasingly tamed. Some people at this stage of practice describe a bubbling feeling of happiness and increased clarity with respect to the true nature of life and all phenomena.

The sixth stage of practice is called "riding the ox home," and in another, more modern era, might be known as rounding third base toward home. Here, the end of the monumental struggle of the past several years, from stages one through five, is somewhat within sight. Mindfulness and the ability to be in the present moment comes with much greater ease.

In the seventh stage of practice, sometimes known as "self alone, ox forgotten," the student—along with his or her ox/ego—has reached home. Here, the self is said to have become forgotten, and the practice is effortless. Moreover, a student in this stage has the ability to express great consideration and compassion for others.

The eighth stage of Zen practice is called "both self and ox transcended." In this stage, it's said that the student realizes that neither the self, which has been seeking, nor the ox, or ego—the object of the search, actually have ever existed!

The ninth stage is known as "reaching the source," and by this stage the practitioner is said to be unconcerned within or without. The notion of duality—light and dark, right and wrong, gain and loss, or life and death—has been vanquished. Both devoted monks and experienced lay students are said to be able to attain this stage of practice.

Finally, the tenth stage—"returning to the marketplace"—literally marks the return of the now-enlightened and compassionate student to the common world. It marks the irrepressible desire of the enlightened individual to share his or her Buddhist teachings with others and to help cause them to seek enlightenment.

By now, it would be said that the "mind-to-mind" transmission of Buddhahood has taken place. The student is recognized as a master, and like Mahakasyapa, he or she has inherited, wordlessly, both the lifeblood of the teachings and direct, personal, and experiential enlightenment. Such masters are one with themselves, with their masters, with all the Zen masters and Buddhas throughout eternity. This life state, of course, is far beyond a simple mastering of meditation. It isn't even the means toward enlightenment but considered to be enlightenment itself. It is the state of life that Zen calls satori. D.T. Suzuki describes satori as "the sudden flashing into consciousness of a new truth hitherto undreamed of. It is a sort of mental catastrophe taking place all at once, after much piling up of matters intellectual and demonstrative. The piling has reached a limit of stability and the whole edifice has come tumbling to the ground, when, behold, a new heaven is open to full survey."

Zen Sutras and Koans

Master Dogen, the thirteenth-century founder of the Soto school of Zen, called zazen the manifestation of ultimate reality:

> Cease from the practice of intellectual understanding, pursuing words and following after speech, and learn the backward step that turns your light inward to illuminate yourself. Body and mind of themselves will drop away and your original face will be manifested. If you want to attain suchness, you should practice suchness without delay. Cease all movements of the conscious mind, the gauging of all thoughts and views. . . . If you concentrate your efforts single-mindedly, that in itself is negotiating the Way.

To master zazen is to master the self. More to the point, to master zazen is to know that there is no self, or at least no separation between the self and any external phenomena. A master of Zen is said to have accomplished the realization of a state of life in which the body and the mind, according to Master Dogen, "has fallen away."

The accomplishment of such a state, of course, is arduous, and it entails many years of dedicated practice. It requires a mentor. Moreover, that's why, along with devotion to zazen, Zen Buddhism incorporates the recitation of a liturgy, as well as the contemplation of koans.

Each Buddhist school has its own rituals, and liturgy—or a customary public worship—is an important ritual meant to underscore the collective experience of the practitioners, or the sangha, and remind them of the ideal goal that their practice seeks. It's an expression of how the world, ideally, should be. It's a demonstration of perfection, through prayer, meant to remind the practitioners of the hope that their practice promises.

Just as the Roman Catholic liturgy was, until relatively recently, always performed in Latin, Jewish liturgies in Hebrew, and Muslim ones in Arabic, most Buddhist liturgies are recited in the language during which the respective school predominantly flowered. By now, most Zen liturgies recited in the United States tend to be in the English language. At the Zen Mountain Monastery in upstate New York, for example, the daily liturgies include the Prajna Paramita Heart Sutra, which dates back some two thousand years to the first century, as well as a Meal Gatha. The recitation of the Heart Sutra, in particular, can be beautiful and stirring, accompanied as it is with burning incense, tinkling bells and beating drums, the beats becoming faster and faster as the congregation recites, in English, the various negatives used to point toward an expression of emptiness:

No sensation, conception, discrimination, awareness
No eye, ear, nose, tongue, body, mind
No color, sound, smell, taste, touch, phenomena
No realm of sight, no realm of consciousness
No ignorance and no end to ignorance
No old age and death and no end to old age and death

No suffering, no cause of suffering
No extinguishing, no path
No wisdom and no gain

Yet as perplexing, even in English, as the Heart Sutra's description of emptiness might be, the meaning of Zen koans are even further beyond logical comprehension.

The several volumes of collected Zen koans are meant to be tools used to assist the practitioner of zazen in achieving enlightenment. Each koan is presented either as a riddle or as a brief, evidently nonsensical, exchange between an old master and student. The koan is framed as an attempt to open a practitioner's mind beyond its semblance of rational thinking in order to allow that practitioner to see the true reality of life. Accordingly, Zen and its koans, along with a huge inventory of supporting Zen stories and anecdotes, presumes that the world as viewed by most of us walking blindly through our daily lives is delusional. The koan is a prompt that forces the Zen student over the precipice of rationality so that his or her mind is compelled to consider the true reality within.

One of the more famous koans is set forth as an exchange between Yeno, the Sixth Patriarch of Zen, and a student, who had asked him what Zen was. Yeno replied: "When your mind is not dwelling on the dualism of good and evil, what is your original face before you were born?" On the one hand, this koan is meant to awaken students to the fact that their former ways of looking at things were not necessarily correct. A more advanced student, however, may recognize the "original face" to be his or her true inner self.

By design, of course, there is no right answer to a koan, and there's also no way to describe what they really mean. Again, Zen is experiential; the value of the koan is not truly revealed unless the student is engaged in a deep practice of zazen. The koans seek to halt the incessant, rational thoughts that each of us has. They short-circuit our logical thought processes, cause doubt, and set forth impossible challenges. Only then, when, in the words of D.T. Suzuki, you throw yourself "directly and unreservedly against the iron wall of the koan," is an unexpected region of the mind revealed.

Nevertheless, to the uninitiated, many Zen anecdotes appear to relate gratuitously violent stories that border on Three Stooges humor. One involves a student, Hyakujo, who was out one day with his master, Baso, when they observed a flock of wild geese flying.

"What are they?" asked Baso.

"They are wild geese, sir."

"To where are they flying?"

"They have flown away."

Then Baso, who thereafter had taken hold of Hyakujo's nose and gave it such a twist that Hyakujo cried out in pain, said: "You say they have flown away, but all the same they have been here from the very first." Hyakujo then instantly achieved satori.

Another famous nose-pulling story goes like this:

Sekkyo asked one of his accomplished monks, "Can you take hold of empty space?"

"Yes, sir."

"Show me how you do it."

The monk stretched out his arm and clutched at empty space.

"Is that the way?" asked the master. "But after all you have not got anything."

"What then," asked the monk, "is your way?"

Sekkyo immediately took hold of the monk's nose and gave it a hard pull, which caused the monk to exclaim, "Oh, oh, how hard you pull at my nose! You are hurting me terribly!"

"That is the way to have good hold of empty space," said the master.

Other Zen lessons, which one hopes are apocryphal, involve cutting off the finger of a child, cutting a stray cat in two, and throwing an acolyte off of a porch some several feet above the ground.

Although entertaining from a voyeuristic perspective, the point of all of these stories is not to condone violence but to free a Zen student's mind from the bondage of logic. These blows and shouts, especially in the Rinzai tradition of Zen, are designed to suddenly awaken the subject of the attack to the sublime realm of emptiness. Such a practice, accordingly, is not for anyone fainthearted or mentally unstable.

At the same time, these more brutal anecdotes bring into focus the question of ethics in a practice that seeks to dispense with logic. According to Zen, logic is self-conscious and thus an obstacle to reaching enlightenment and satori. But if logic is irrelevant, so then is ethics, which is the application of logic to the facts of life. If good, ethical deeds are inherently motivated by self-conscious behavior, which, to some extent, they certainly are, then Zen might say that a charitable person's mind is not pure. Zen does not want to be bound by rules, it wants its practitioners to realize their own truths and, in a sense, create their own rules. While violence is not at all characteristic of American Zen, which is a rather peace-loving community, the history of Zen violence, most notable in World War II, and in the Zen koans and tales of yore, is symptomatic, perhaps, of the pitfalls of detachment from logic and ethics.

Are such observations the result of too much thinking? After all, each of us knows relatively unhappy people who nevertheless love to point out everyone else's shortcomings. And it's always preferable to be happy than correct, isn't it? Zen trains one to not be distracted, to never pull away from the joy and reality of the present moment. It's not a rational process but rather an experiential one. Better then to just do it, and stop all of this silly thinking.

6

Tantric Sects:
Merit, Meditation, and Mentoring in Tibetan Buddhism

Vajrayana Buddhism, of which Tibetan Buddhism is the best-known example in America today, represents a "newer" movement in the faith—dating from the seventh century, well over a thousand years after Shakyamuni Buddha lived and taught. Its scriptures, known as *tantra*, are distinct from the traditional sutras. It's neither Theravada nor Mahayana Buddhism, but a blend of the two with a third tradition—Vajrayana—considered by its practitioners to be paramount to either. Unlike traditional Theravada (also known historically as Hinayana), Vajrayana rituals promise the achievement of enlightenment within this lifetime. And unlike Mahayana, at least up until the thirteenth century, Vajrayana alone set forth the possibility of doing so without the very many traditional stages of bodhisattva ascendency. This was a revolutionary development in Buddhism. This Vajrayana approach to realizing enlightenment in one lifetime historically foreshadowed the foundation for the later philosophical emphasis by Zen Master Dogen on zazen, as well as the teaching by Nichiren of chanting *Nam-myoho-renge-kyo*—both of which likewise promise enlightenment within one's current life. Accordingly, Vajrayana Buddhism upended the vision of how a practitioner must go about achieving enlightenment in many Mahayana schools, and it was a forerunner to later perspectives that reformed the Mahayana traditions.

Vajra means "diamond," or, in other words, something indestructible. It also means "thunderbolt," connoting a supremely effective or irresistible practice of faith. Another word for Vajrayana Buddhism is Tantric Buddhism, with its emphasis on the Buddhist tantra teachings, rituals, practice, and realization.

Since the twentieth century, the word tantra has been associated for the most part with tantric sex. Although some Buddhist tantras utilize male and female metaphors to demonstrate principles of weaving together the physical and spiritual, it's off the mark to think that Vajrayana, or Tantric, Buddhism is in some way about sexual best practices. Like Zen, Vajrayana Buddhism sets forth a serious quest for enlightenment.

Tibetan Buddhism, as a branch of Vajrayana, is among the more complex of the Buddhist schools flourishing in America. As with the other major Buddhist sects, there's a prominent emphasis on practice and mentoring, but in addition, Tibetan Buddhism stresses study and a deep understanding of Buddhist philosophy and cosmology as an integral aspect of the practice. Supernatural beings have key roles in Tibetan Buddhism. Both benevolent bodhisattvas and wrathful deities abound, and spirits derived from the earlier Tibetan nativist Bon religion continue to prosper in the faith. Such a rich and poetic metaphysical context has inspired in Tibetan Buddhism a strong artistic tradition. Exquisitely expressive paintings, prayer wheels, flags, and other graphic representations are often used as aids to understanding and reminders of the spirit world within our physical domain.

Tibetan Buddhism includes innumerable treatises, meditation methods, deities, principles, practices, and traditions, and without a guide or teacher, it's very difficult, if not impossible, to sort out which might be best for you. There are four major Tibetan Buddhist sects, all of which somewhat differ. There is an ever-expanding Tibetan Buddhist-related meditation school known as Shambhala, which is very popular in North America. It takes a long time to read and comprehend Tibetan Buddhism's key scriptures, which is why, in part, the school places an essential emphasis on having a teacher or *lama* that can personally assist you in your practice. It's one thing to read the works of the Dalai Lama and appreciate the basic principles of this philosophy, but quite another to embrace and actually practice its teachings over a lifetime. The correct practice of Tibetan Buddhism requires intellect, discipline, devotion, and a considerable period of training.

Tibetan Buddhism is concerned with how to live in and be of benefit to the world. It's about how to be skillful in life. Tibetan Buddhism, like other Buddhist traditions, considers everyone to have a Buddha nature, or a basic goodness. The control of ego—and not specifically the achievement of happiness—is the particular goal of this faith.

The experiences of the mind are what keep most of us moving forward through life. Such experiences include all those resulting in happiness, joy, suffering, and pain. The mind, naturally, is preoccupied moment by moment with the effort to negotiate its way through these events and emotions. Tibetan Buddhism seeks to provide a philosophical and practical road map with respect to how one can be free from all these vicissitudes, particularly those relating to pain and suffering.

Tibetan Buddhism teaches that people are the same at their essence and not distinguished by outside characteristics. All people feel alone when they suffer. But Tibetan Buddhism suggests that these feelings of isolation or separation are not functions of the suffering itself but rather misunderstandings of not seeing the truth. Hopelessness comes from such isolation and alienation. Accordingly, Tibetan Buddhist training helps a practitioner to let go of misunderstanding in order to achieve a transformation into a sensitive, genuine, and enlightened person. Such Vajrayana practice is considered the pinnacle of Tibetan Buddhism and constitutes the primary daily practice. And this practice of compassion, known to Tibetan Buddhists as *bodhicitta*, is what gives rise to one's ultimate enlightenment.

Buddhist Tolerance

"Merit," or what some other Buddhists might call "good karma," manifests positive external conditions. One's merit derives from past lives and a present goodness that acknowledges everyone's respective Buddha nature. Cultivating merit decreases our self-ego, as well as our self-centeredness and suffering. It diminishes our attachment and inclinations toward aggression. From a Tibetan Buddhist perspective, the absence of negativity is peace. Without merit, there can be no peace of mind.

The true meaning of life, as most Buddhists would agree, is not how far one has advanced in a career or how many worldly possessions are collected, but how profoundly an individual has contributed to others. Enlightenment, however defined, is the aim of most Buddhist practitioners. In order to achieve this, of course, and in order to prepare the foundation for happiness, a person has to first secure peace within him- or herself. Tibetan Buddhism encourages its practitioners to establish such inner peace by developing a sensitive mind and care toward others. And it views the external manifestation of such peace as tolerance.

Tibetan Buddhism holds that a strong heart can bear and be immune to pain. But this is only developed through tolerance. We tolerated birth through a narrow birth canal, so we must have the capacity to also tolerate sickness, old age, and death. Moreover, Tibetan Buddhism places a great value on the cultivation of nonviolence toward the outside world. Tibetan Buddhists are encouraged to not be provoked by others who cause them to be aggressive. At its essence, nonviolence is to know that tolerance is the only solution, and that the means to achieve this is to bear the pain. We increase our inner strength to the extent we can bear such pain. The challenge, and the greatest purification of all, is the opportunity to grow strong and to welcome pain with a positive attitude. As a result of such a practice, one ultimately becomes fearless.

Tibetan Buddhists need look no further than to Tibet for examples of such tolerance and Buddhist forbearance. Human rights organizations have documented far too many instances of Buddhist monks and nuns who had been tortured and murdered by the occupying Chinese military. Moreover, thousands of monasteries in Tibet were ransacked during the 1959 invasion of Tibet, which ultimately forced the exile to India of the Dalai Lama and many other leading Tibetan Buddhist lamas. Such resistance, both through nonviolent—and, more recently—violent means, continues to the present day.

From the Tibetan Buddhist view, tolerance is not exclusively a political means. A practitioner must develop tolerance toward his or her own confusion and weaknesses. In other words, a student ought to discern them but not indulge them. There should be no excuses based on mood, ailments, or any justifications if one wants to achieve inner peace. Tolerance suggests forgiveness to others for their mistakes and forgiveness to oneself as well.

The *Middle Way* is a Buddhist concept that most people understand as living a balanced life. Traditionally, it's a life lived between the extremes of self-indulgence and self-denial. In this sense, the Tibetan Buddhist view of peace and tolerance can be expressed as neither giving up nor giving in. Not giving up requires being kind to oneself. But tolerance and patience is not passivity. It requires a strong mind. And it requires overcoming the pain of self-importance.

The self wants to believe that everything is permanent, but it is not. It does this in order to preserve its own obsession to be permanent. The truth, according to Tibetan Buddhism, is that a pure state of mind can only be realized by achieving indestructible inner peace. This is a process, of course, that takes time, wisdom, and a skillful mind.

Tibetan Buddhism emphasizes rituals pertaining to body, speech, and mind. These correspond to *mudra*, *mantra*, and *mandala*, respectively, in the context of specific practices.

As seen as part of the Zen practice of zazen, mudra is a way of holding one's hands and fingers during meditation. A mudra is said to guide energy flow and reflexes to the brain. In a Buddhist context, it represents the universal power of enlightenment, although different mudras can represent different aspects. Some indicate an absence of fear, others compassion and charity, and still others are said to expel demons.

A mantra is a word or a phrase that, when chanted or meditated upon, brings about spiritual transformation. It connects the practitioner with the ultimate law of the universe and assists in the achievement of enlightenment. Perhaps the most famous example of a mantra is "Om," which is not Buddhist but derived from Hinduism.

Finally, a mandala is a physical representation of the Buddha's enlightenment. Mandalas are sometimes objects, like statues, or often also scrolls upon which illustrations, mantras, or other characters meant to symbolize enlightenment may be written. The practitioner is instructed to focus his or her attention on the mandala while reciting the mantra to stimulate and harness the mystical power of the universe and thus enter the realm of enlightenment.

These rituals, and the tools that support them, are the means toward walking the three principle stages of the Tibetan Buddhist path: renunciation of the suffering, *samsara* world; the altruistic wish to attain enlightenment; and the wisdom to realize emptiness.

To achieve this, Tibetan Buddhism prescribes mentoring, meditation, and study.

Mentoring

As with all forms of Buddhism, a practitioner's relationship to his or her mentor is critical to the quest for enlightenment. In Tibetan Buddhism, in particular, a personal relationship with a teacher is a precondition for entry into the practice. This requires of the student much more than a desire to "check out" Buddhist practice. Instead, this relationship is meant to last an entire lifetime (if not more) and can only be broken by the teacher or the student after some very grave offense. Perhaps more so even than the mentor-student relationship in Zen or Soka Gakkai Buddhism, the practice of Tibetan Buddhism requires total trust and devotion to the mentor. It is the heart of the teaching. Complete confidence in and union with the mentor—known to practitioners as *guru yoga*—is considered indispensible to the attainment of enlightenment. It is so critical, in fact, that the mentor is to be regarded as even more important than the Buddha. Whereas the Buddha may be compared to the sun, the contemporaneous teacher, or *guru* or *lama*, in Tibetan Buddhism has been described as a magnifying glass without which the power of the sun could not be harnessed to strike a fire. The mentoring relationship in Tibetan Buddhism is meant to be a deeply personal and intimate relationship in faith. Devotion to the mentor is seen as the surest and fastest way to achieve enlightenment.

The idea, in part, behind such utter dedication to the teacher is that a Buddha like Shakyamuni lived some 2,600 years ago and that today's practitioners, clouded as they are in these defiled times, require the opportunity to meet someone who can personally pull them out of their benighted worlds. Since one's respective guru is here in this world, with the student, and since his enlightenment, according to Tibetan Buddhism, is equal to that of Shakyamuni, Guru Rinpoche, and all other Buddhas, his kindness actually exceeds that of his predecessors because he is manifest here in this lifetime.

The practice of guru yoga has four methods: outer, inner, secret, and most secret. The outer method is to visualize the guru dwelling above one's head and to pray to him with intense devotion. The inner method is to realize, through meditation and practice, that one's own body, speech, and mind are inseparable from those of the guru's. The secret method is to meditate upon the guru in what is referred to as his form of divine enjoyment. And the most secret method involves meditating on a state of awareness focused on what Tantric Buddhism considers to be the primordial Buddha. At its essence, the practice of guru yoga is to remember the teacher in all of one's moment-by-moment activities.

It takes strong faith to accomplish this. First, the student has to seek out and find a fully realized teacher and attend to him—or, sometimes, her—with total confidence. Moreover, that student must come to the realization that there is no separation between his or her mentor and the enlightenment of Shakyamuni or Guru Rinpoche. In the tradition of Vajrayana Buddhism, therefore, there is no one who achieved enlightenment without having devoted him or herself first to a spiritual teacher.

To find a good mentor, many Tibetan Buddhists observe that one should hang out on the edges, and then pull away and come back. It's up to the student to decide and investigate, and it should be a lengthy process because the relationship, once initiated, is meant to last forever. Some recommend that the person with whom one chooses to study should already embody what the student, himself, is seeking. Doubt is to be encouraged, and the student is often very skeptical before selecting a Tibetan Buddhist teacher, many of whom, at least in America, tend to exhibit wry, sarcastic, and lighthearted natures.

Once the relationship is permanently established, however, the mentor acts like a mirror. The mentor will provide personal instruction and custom-designed practices for the practitioner, based on what the mentor sees within the practitioner's life and what is most required for that person to negotiate his or her respective path toward enlightenment. Such rituals might include specific mantras, meditation methods, mandalas, mudras, or even a series of prostrations.

Tibetan Buddhists show respect toward their faith when entering or leaving a prayer room containing a mandala. When in the presence of a lama or teacher, the practitioner is expected to bow. After the lama is seated, practitioners will perform three formal prostrations as a sign of respect to the teacher.

As with Zen and Soka Gakkai Buddhist practices, the basic entry to practice is the acceptance that we each have a Buddha nature, or the state of enlightenment, already present within our lives. In the case of us ordinary individuals, however, it's not recognized, and so we need to practice in order to manifest it.

Meditation

Meditation in Tibetan Buddhism is the vehicle to develop and harness one's enlightened nature. It allows one to gain perspective on his or her emotions. It leads one to be rid of attachment but not desire. Happiness, in Tibetan Buddhism, is not particularly the goal. Rather, the practice of meditation is more about developing an intellectually accurate map about the development of the mind. Moments of clarity and wakefulness come in occasional flashes and are not meant to be permanent. What is key is clarity about the impermanence of the self.

Tibetan Buddhist meditation always stresses the importance of *bodhicitta*, a state of life in which one is awakened and has profound compassion toward all living beings. Accordingly, every act and thought should be motivated by the unparalleled altruism of wanting to see all people enlightened. If that's our motivation, according to these teachings, then whether or not we succeed, we ourselves experience the benefits of this sincere, compassionate attitude. The Dalai Lama has spoken often of what he refers to as "wise selfishness." What it means, essentially, is that human nature is inherently selfish, so if a practitioner recognizes that the quickest way to get the things he or she wants is by helping others, then go ahead and engage in such a selfishly compassionate practice. It's a paradox also embraced by Soka Gakkai members, among others: if you want personal happiness then devote yourself to others.

This me-first attitude toward something as quintessentially egoless as compassion has a unique appeal to Americans. If our prayer or meditation is focused on selfish desires—getting that new house, for example—it won't work. In fact, a focus on worldly benefits and possessions, even while meditating, will leave a negative cause in our lives and prolong our suffering. And since the aim of Buddhism is to transcend suffering, that's not the best way to proceed. Instead, the practitioner ought to take that desire and transform it into something compassionate. Maybe in this case a practitioner desires that new house so more of his fellow Buddhists would have a place to congregate. If he meditates on that house with a sincere desire to help the Buddhist sangha, for example, then the motivation behind that prayer is closer to that of bodhicitta. The benefit of his thought and action, in this case, isn't determined by the thought or action itself but by the underlying motivation. This shouldn't be confused with real bodhisattva practice, and the profound altruism that it entails, but it's certainly a good step in the direction of learning how to develop compassion toward others. Whatever our desire, we should contemplate the suffering of others and want to relieve that suffering. Everything, then, can be transformed. Or, in Buddhist parlance, poison is transformed into medicine.

Tibetan Buddhism describes two different approaches to meditation: analytical and concentrated. Analytical meditation is recommended as the first approach for a beginner who is considering the practice of Buddhism as a spiritual path. With this approach, which is closer to careful consideration than it is to actual meditation, a person uses the power of analytical reasoning to gauge the value of the teaching and to determine whether or not it appears to be true. As with the selection of a mentor, even the initiation of the beginning stage of practice ought to take some time. There is no push or tradition of urgent proselytization in Tibetan Buddhism. The analytical meditation method encourages the beginner to read about the tenets of the faith and to make a firm determination with respect to whether he or she wants to read more—or whether it's a bunch of hogwash. The more time we spend analyzing, and the more secure we are in wanting to practice, then the deeper our faith will be and the more effectively our practice will develop. A strong analytical determination will assist when we later meet obstacles in faith. It is the first step in Tibetan Buddhism toward forging a conviction in faith.

On the other hand, concentrated meditation is precisely what we imagine when we think of someone meditating. For example, it's what zazen is for Zen Buddhists. Concentrated meditation is to focus the mind on an object, a thought, or a breath until the mind can be still of ephemeral thoughts and concentrate on it with ease. It occurs when we're trained well enough in a meditation technique so that we can quiet our minds and meditate with stability, not flitting here and there with each and every thought. Although the analytical and concentrated methods are very different, each supports the other. The more we reason, the stronger our efforts will be to practice. And the better our concentration, the keener our powers of logical deduction will become.

Tibetan Buddhism encourages several methods of meditation within the category of concentrated meditation. These include, among others, mindfulness, visualization and *tonglen* practice. Although one's teacher will provide a practitioner with the method that's best for him or her, traditional Tibetan Buddhist centers tend to begin with visualization and mantra practices, while the Shambhala centers, as well as Zen, as we have seen, emphasize a mindfulness practice with beginning students.

The mindfulness meditation approach in Tibetan Buddhism is similar to that of zazen, but it is called *zhinay*, a Tibetan expression for "calm abiding." This method usually starts with a focus on learning how to properly breathe— in a sense, a warm-up for the meditation to come.

As with zazen, sit cross-legged on the floor, preferably in a lotus or half-lotus position, with a pillow as a cushion. The back should be very straight, and the shoulders relaxed, even, and parallel to the floor. The arms are slightly bent, with the forearms resting on one's thighs. The hands, which are on the lap, are positioned palms upward with the tips of the thumbs touching—like the mudra position in Zen. One's chin is tucked in, and the neck is bent a little bit forward. The eyes and mouth are either lightly closed or slightly open, and the tongue touches the roof of one's mouth behind the front teeth. Practitioners will concentrate on a point somewhat in front of them, on the floor, perhaps three or four feet from where they sit.

One will begin, perhaps with a mantra provided by one's teacher, but with the intent always on bodhicitta, contemplating how to reach enlightenment and help all other people achieve the same. Focus on the breath, and bring the mind right to the nose so that it becomes possible to sense the air entering and leaving the body. When a stray thought comes to mind, even if it concerns one's breathing, let it go and focus again on the meditation. Some beginners, as with Zen, count their breaths, but others concentrate on a mantra. When distracted, refocus and come back to the breath.

This practice of zhinay builds a stable and strong focus that serves as the foundation for comprehending the very nature of the mind. This insight into the reality of "how things are" allows *mahamudra* to be revealed—a state of enlightenment free from delusion, contrivance, or even effort. The stillness of mind that one achieves is compared to the image of a candle flame flickering in the breeze, which becomes still if surrounded by a glass chimney, which enables it to burn steadily. Zhinay, like zazen for Zen Buddhists, is considered in Tibetan Buddhism the bedrock from which all spiritual enlightenment springs.

Visualization is probably the most common of the Tibetan meditation techniques. In the Kagyu tradition of Tibetan Buddhism, for example, this aspect of Tibetan Buddhist practice is systematically presented in the form of the Six Yogas of Naropa: the inner fire, illusory form, dream, luminosity, the intermediate state following death, and transfer of consciousness from one's body. These Six Yogas prepare the way for enlightenment, or mahamudra, which Trungpa Rinpoche once described as "the vividness of phenomena."

With visualization meditation as the means, Tibetan Buddhists seek to fully activate the inherent wisdom and compassion already present within their lives. A practitioner will often engage in "deity yoga," in which he or she is given by their teacher a specific deity to focus on and visualize during meditation. The practice is meant to lead one toward the full realization of emptiness.

Moreover, four classes of tantra are distinguished based on the person's stage of practice. These are action tantra, performance tantra, yoga tantra, and highest yoga tantra. Deity yoga is a form of action tantra. Performance tantra, in turn, involves visualizing oneself as an enlightened being, as well as seeing an image of a deity in front of oneself as a template. In yoga tantra, the practitioner visualizes him- or herself as the deity itself. Finally, in the highest yoga tantra a student develops proficiency in visualization with the help of a mandala. At this final stage, the student experiences a union of bliss and emptiness. This is sometimes depicted as a male-female sexual embrace.

Visualization meditation promises the synchronization of body and mind. And when a person is so synchronized, according to Tibetan Buddhism, then what is experienced is exactly what has occurred—devoid of delusion or erroneous, subjective interpretation. Accordingly, a person who's trained his or her mind to function at this level possesses an unbiased awareness that will lead toward the most appropriate action or response—one that is guided by compassion. It is considered by many practitioners as the recipe for basic sanity.

A third common Tibetan Buddhist meditation method is known as *tonglen*, which literally means "giving and taking." Here, while meditating, the practitioner visualizes breathing in the suffering of another, or others, and breathing out happiness for them. The purpose of the practice is to create positive karma, or merit, by helping other people while diminishing the emphasis on one's own ego. Tonglen meditation is part of the Seven Points of Mind Training, a set of guidelines for bringing negative situations toward the path of meditation and enlightenment. Tonglen practice is more difficult than it sounds, as it can dislodge a lot of emotion as one breathes in suffering and connects to what it is that hurts. Moreover, a tonglen practitioner breathes out what he or she believes is his or her own joy, so one learns to let go of even what tends to inspire or delight. That will shake up anyone's primary attachments.

In support of the meditation practice, Tibetan Buddhists, like Zen and Soka Gakkai Buddhists, recite a daily liturgy. The prayers will differ based on the particular sect or teacher but in general the liturgy is focused on taking refuge in and developing bodhicitta. Other prayers concern the cultivation of the four immeasurable attributes of love, compassion, joy, and equanimity. Portions of the Diamond or Heart Sutras may be recited, and mantras dedicated to past great Vajrayana masters also will be offered. When a large group is gathered together, prayer sheets containing the liturgy are generally offered to all participants.

Lamrim and the Tibetan Book of the Dead

Tibetan Buddhism, as compared to Zen, or in some respects even the Soka Gakkai, places a great emphasis on study. Where all claim to be experiential faiths, Vajrayana Buddhism, with its rich literature, nevertheless bases its practice on a well-developed doctrinal ground.

The *lamrim* are the texts studied by most Tibetan Buddhists, and they describe in detail the stages of enlightenment. Most interpretations of lamrim are based on an eleventh-century writing by a monk named Atisa. Those teachings, in turn, inspired Je Tsongkhapa's *Lamrim Chenmo*, a fourteenth-century treatise that became a major text of the Geluk school. Tibetan Buddhists believe that the lamrim are based on the sutras taught by Shakyamuni. The lamrim explain karma, rebirth, Buddhist cosmology, and meditation practices.

The lamrim divide Buddhist practitioners into three groups: people of modest scope, who search for happiness within the samsara world; people of medium scope, who seek inner peace and abandon worldly pleasures; and people of high scope, who use all means to relieve the suffering of all people. The lamrim describe the all-important concept of bodhicitta, the state in which one strives to achieve Buddhahood. One who practices bodhicitta, in turn, is a bodhisattva.

Among the lamrim's most basic teachings is the moral practice of resistance to the ten nonvirtuous acts. This ethical code is also known as the Ten Precepts:

- *Killing any living being (including by abortion or suicide).*
- *Stealing anything of value.*
- *Adultery, or sexual misconduct.*
- *Lying.*

- *Divisive talk.*
- *Harsh talk.*
- *Idle talk, or gossip.*
- *Coveting the possessions or personal qualities of others.*
- *Harboring ill will toward others.*
- *Having an incorrect worldview, or a view that fails to recognize karma as the direct cause of all experience.*

Perhaps the most famous of the Tibetan treatises is the *Bardo Thodol*, Anglicized as the *Tibetan Book of the Dead*. This discourse is said to be one of the many termas hidden centuries ago by Guru Rinpoche. It was reportedly discovered by a lama in the fourteenth century, and it gained worldwide renown when translated into English and first published in 1927. The text sets out to describe the experiences that the consciousness has after death, and it seeks to guide one through those experiences. According to the text, the intermediate period between death and either rebirth or nirvana—the *bardo*, in Tibetan— is forty-nine days. The *Bardo Thodol* includes meditation instructions, visualizations of deities, liturgies and prayers, lists of mantras, descriptions of the signs of death, and indications of future rebirth to be employed as death approaches. It also includes prayers and meditations to be offered to support the deceased's enlightenment or well-being in the after-death state. The prayers are meant to be recited and the rituals to be performed by teachers, friends, and loved ones as death is closing in, or after it has occurred.

The focus of the *Bardo Thodol* is the attainment of enlightenment at death. The text distinguishes three stages of death. The first stage is the moment of death. At this moment a person's only avail is sincere religious practice. Also at this moment, where both the physical elements of life, as well as thoughts and emotions cease, we are left with our original Buddha nature, what Tibetan Buddhism calls Ground Luminosity. According to the *Bardo Thodol*, the individual at this moment has two opportunities to recognize this state as his or her true, original self. If, as a result of a lifetime of devoted Buddhist practice, he or she does recognize this self, then he or she will proceed to a state of nirvana, or eternal bliss and happiness.

These flashes, perhaps, can be compared to the shining light or the greetings by angels or other religious icons that some people with near-death experiences have reported. Who knows? It may be that what the spirit perceives at the moment of death takes the form of the respective religious teachers that were impressed on us during our corporeal lives.

In any case, if the Ground Luminosity isn't recognized, according to Tibetan Buddhism, then a second stage of recognition, the Body of Bliss, another manifestation of Buddha nature, occurs. If still the spirit fails to recognize this state, then it will, in the bardo state, begin to again acknowledge the familiar sights and sounds of life: tastes, smells, sounds and other senses of existence. The consciousness then begins to yearn for rebirth, and the soul is thus prepared to enter and enliven the spirit of a newly conceived physical life at the instantaneous moment of conception. Whether that life is to be born into pleasant or unpleasant circumstances is a function of the collective karma of that soul—the causes one has made throughout lifetime after lifetime. One's next life, therefore, is a reflection of the predominant condition of life manifest at one's death.

Of course, the point to what might seems like an obsession with death is how to live one's life. Suffering is one of the Four Noble Truths. But since there is an origin to suffering, it can be overcome, and one can move forward from there. The recognition that everything is impermanent, and thus subject to change, is critical to understanding that even suffering can change.

Buddhism places a paramount emphasis on learning how to live within the present moment. And although Zen, more than other schools, tends to have an exclusive focus on the present moment with little regard for such notions as an afterlife or reincarnation, Tibetan Buddhism and the Soka Gakkai are very much concerned with death as a means toward learning how to best live. If we take nothing but our karma with us, it's self-evident that we'll need to live the best life, and make the best causes, that we can while blessed with the wondrous state of life. And where Zen points to zazen as the key to unlock one's Buddha nature, and the Soka Gakkai the chanting of *Nam-myoho-renge-kyo*, Tibetan Buddhists utilize meditation, visualization, and self-reflection.

Buddhist Deities

An intriguing and creative aspect of Tibetan Buddhism, particularly from an artistic point of view, is its pantheon of dozens of deities, or spiritual essences. These entities aren't gods in a polytheistic sense but rather represent aspects of

Fresco of a Mahakala, a Tibetan Buddhist wrathful deity, at Alchi Monastery in India.

enlightenment. They are used at times as devotional tools for the practitioner to visualize during meditation in order to help actualize a particular aspect of enlightenment that he or she is seeking. Over the centuries, artists have produced extraordinary images of these figures, with the so-called "wrathful deities" standing for the very best portraits.

Some of the more spectacular images include Chakrasamvara, the supreme Vajrayana meditational deity, who is blue, with four faces and twelve arms, depicted in an embrace with his Wisdom Consort Vajravarahi, symbolizing the union of wisdom and skillful means; the lionlike Mahakala, a wrathful deity who destroys chatter and brings the practitioner's mind back to attentive focus; or Vajrakilaya, who wears a crown of skulls and is depicted in flames.

Veneration of the deities does not constitute the main practice of Tibetan Buddhism. Still, they're considered useful to help practitioners to focus and to become familiar with Vajrayana cosmology.

Shambhala

Shambhala, or Shambhala Buddhism, is a somewhat simplified branch of Tibetan Buddhism, founded by Chogyam Trungpa Rinpoche, that blends traditional meditation techniques with Tibetan nativist study and practice of the way of a spiritual warrior. More specifically, it's a union of the Kagyu and Nyingma schools of Tibetan Buddhism with the Shambhala philosophy introduced by Trungpa Rinpoche in the 1970s and expressed in his book *Shambhala: The Sacred Path of the Warrior*. His teachings during this period, and as expressed in his work, sought to establish the best gateway to introduce Westerners to the teachings of Tibetan Buddhism and to the concept, specifically, of Shambhala. The warrior aspect of the training is not militaristic. Rather, it's said to be based on the tradition of Tibet's King Gesar, a folkloric figure held to be an emanation of Guru Rinpoche. Shambhala, whether intentional or not, has become the main portal in the United States through which beginners enter the world of Tibetan Buddhism. Its leader is Trungpa Rinpoche's son and spiritual heir, Sakyong Mipham Rinpoche.

In Shambhala, every person is seen to possess a fundamental nature of goodness, warmth, and intelligence. This nature can be developed and become manifest through meditation and then projected into daily life so that it positively influences family, friends, and the community at large. This journey of awakening to cut through the fear and egotism that dominate modern life requires the training of a spiritual warrior—it takes a concentrated focus on kindness, courage, and conviction to cut through any fear.

Trungpa Rinpoche believed that people could uplift themselves through developing a keen appreciation for their own lives, as well as the interconnected lives we each share. This path of the Shambhala warrior is blazed only by honestly looking within one's heart, which is accomplished through mindfulness meditation. Shambhala promises its practitioners the ability to view the world as one full of pureness and beauty. Once body and mind are synchronized, and arrogance is crushed, a person is able to express consideration and compassion for others in the world. The goal of such training, according to Trungpa Rinpoche, is a basic "sanity." Shambhala literature somewhat soft-sells the relation of its programs to the practice of Buddhism and rather emphasizes Shambhala's openness to people of any faith, without any contradiction with respect to whatever preexisting beliefs they may hold. Still, its current leader, Sakyong Mipham, has a clear vision of what Shambhala promises:

> In essence, the emphasis of the Buddhist path is to help us attain enlightenment, and the emphasis of the Shambhala path is to help us create and maintain a good society. When we put these two together, we have the Shambhalian Buddhist view of enlightened society. Thus the two paths work in tandem, not in competition.

At its core, Shambhala training consists of contemplative workshops with an aim toward nurturing mindfulness and self-awareness. As with all Vajrayana traditions, meditation is seen as the key to strengthening the mind. In the founder's words, "Shambhala vision is not purely a philosophy. It is actually training yourself to be a warrior. It is learning to treat yourself better, so that you can help to build an enlightened society." The program is inspired by Trungpa Rinpoche's vision of the historical and legendary Shambhala—a mythical Buddhist pure land said to be both peaceful and fearless, which, in his view, belongs neither to East nor West. It is designed for the lay practitioner— there are no monks to be ordained, and students are encouraged to take the principles learned in the practice and apply them to family, career, and all aspects of life.

Programs offered in the Shambhala tradition are concerned with how to cultivate the Great Eastern Sun, or the primordial energy and brilliance said to be the basis for all that exists. "Raising windhorse" is a practice meant to develop strong life force, which also opens a person's heart and refreshes their confidence. "Drala" is the elemental and magical strength inherent in the world. The development of drala promises "unchangingness," or the ability to have no second thoughts—what Trungpa Rinpoche called a "flickering mind." Drala incorporates the primordial energy of the Great Eastern Sun, the unchangingness of a warrior, and a third element: bravery.

Shambhala practice also incorporates study of the "four dignities"—meek, perky, outrageous, and inscrutable. Meek concerns the humble beginning stages of a warrior's journey, and it is an antidote to arrogance. Perky is the cultivation of a vibrant inner energy. The development of outrageous and inscrutable skills are said to assist the warrior in overcoming the fear of making mistakes.

The "Warrior Assembly," which Shambhala refers to as the jewel of its training, is a teaching aimed at learning how to create an enlightened society. Participants receive in this training the transmission of advanced Shambhala warrior practices. It includes study of an important Shambhala text known as *The Golden Sun of the Great East*, which is believed to enable one to transform confusion and hesitation into wisdom and authenticity.

Diamond Mountain University and Retreat Center

Diamond Mountain University, in Arizona, is a nontraditional Tibetan Buddhist school and retreat founded by Michael Roach, who was ordained as a Geluk monk and became the first American to qualify as a Geshe— an honorific title indicating the achievement of a high academic degree for monastics.

In the late 1990s, Roach married one of his most devoted students, Christine McNally, which caused the Dalai Lama, as well as the Tibetan Buddhist scholar Robert Thurman, to call for him to renounce his monastic vows. Roach did not comply. McNally and her teacher eventually divorced but remained colleagues.

In 2010, Roach and McNally initiated an intensive meditation retreat at Diamond Mountain in which approximately forty practitioners were prohibited, among other restrictive rules, from speaking during the entire three-year duration of the retreat. McNally, by then, had remarried a man named Ian Thorson, who was also her student. Violations of the terms of the retreat reportedly occurred, and Diamond Mountain's board of directors ultimately ordered McNally and Thorson to leave the retreat and the center in February 2012.

McNally and Thorson left the property, but apparently attempted to take refuge in a cave on nearby, deserted Bureau of Land Management property. Thorson died there of dehydration and exposure in April 2012, and McNally, who survived, was discovered delirious and near death.

Some of Roach's former students have since criticized Roach for how the matter was handled and publicly accuse him of authoritarian tactics and dogmatic actions that run counter to the spirit of Buddhism.

Whether or not Roach or Diamond Mountain is responsible for Thorson's unfortunate and probably avoidable death is an open question. But the propriety of running three-year retreats in which no one can openly communicate raises the question of when Buddhism becomes cultlike. Shakyamuni, of course, famously criticized the ascetics of his day for engaging in extreme practices that, prior to his enlightenment under the Bodhi tree, led him nearly to death.

Buddhism, at its heart, is a life science of compassion. What Diamond Mountain runs at its obscure Arizona campus appears to bear little relation to the Buddhist ideals of consideration, compassion, or enlightenment—not to mention normal daily life. Moreover, with respect to Vajrayana practitioners, it offers a big, fat, flashing warning light concerning the importance of carefully and patiently choosing one's mentor.

7

Repeat After Me: *Nam* . . . *Myoho* . . . *Renge* . . . *Kyo*

At first blush, the dharma of the Soka Gakkai is similar that of either Zen or Tibetan Buddhism. The objective of enlightenment is the same, there is study of Buddhist doctrine, there is a mentor, there is a liturgy, and there is a mantra and a mandala. But the methods of prayer employed to achieve an enlightened condition of life are so completely different that adherents of other Buddhist schools have typically never heard of the Soka Gakkai or, if they have, consider it to be something not Buddhist, or at most on the fringes of Buddhism. There is no zazen or even meditation in the Soka Gakkai. There is, instead, chanting. There is no monastery, temple, or clergy. What there is, conspicuously, is the largest and most ethnically diverse denomination of Buddhists in America. And, as with the other American Mahayana Buddhist schools, there is a promise of enlightenment in this lifetime.

Perhaps even more notably, while the philosophical literature underpinning the dharma embraced by the Soka Gakkai is at least as voluminous as that of Zen and Tibetan Buddhism, its prescribed practice is considerably easier and far less expensive for its followers to adhere to.

The Buddhist practice of the Soka Gakkai derives from Nichiren, the thirteenth-century Japanese monk who so traumatized the Japanese political and religious establishment of his day that his teachings are still met with suspicion by some other Buddhist sects and religious scholars. Nichiren, as mentioned previously, caustically denounced his contemporary Zen, Shingon, and Pure Land schools and, in turn, elicited persecution upon himself and his then-small band of devoted followers. Although Nichiren's influence on public affairs gradually waned following his death, and his Buddhist sangha fractured into a number of different schools, his uncompromising spirit toward the practice of Buddhism was rekindled by lay leaders Makiguchi, Toda, and Daisaku Ikeda during a period spanning pre-World War II up until today. These teachings spread more quickly than other Buddhist schools in the United States due, in part, to an emphasis on aggressive propagation from the 1960s through the 1980s. The rah-rah nature of the Soka Gakkai organization in America during that period, coupled with the Soka Gakkai's political activities in Japan at that time, brought the group an intensive and unwelcome level of media scrutiny, much of it predictably negative. The SGI-USA was accused, at times, of cultlike activities, and its inclination through the late 1980s, at Nichiren Shoshu's urging, to not participate in interfaith activities, left the organization isolated within the wider religious community. The SGI-USA was never seen as particularly threatening in any way, but it was also not considered especially mainstream in the world of Buddhism. Meanwhile, its members steadfastly practiced, the organization continued to grow, and it has since been recognized by numerous Buddhist scholars as not only a legitimate Buddhist movement but one that's particularly well-suited for American culture.

Chanting Nam-myoho-renge-kyo

The main practice of Soka Gakkai members is to chant the mantra *Nam-myoho-renge-kyo* to a mandala known as the Gohonzon. *Myoho-renge-kyo* is the title of the Lotus Sutra. Nichiren, after spending many years studying the teachings of all the major Buddhist schools, came to the conclusion, through the insights of Zhiyi, the sixth-century Chinese Buddhist scholar and progenitor of the Tendai school, that the Lotus Sutra was supreme among all of Shakyamuni's teachings. Moreover, as suggested by Zhiyi, the period following Shakyamuni's death was distinguished by the Early, Middle, and Latter Days of the Law. These designations correspond to roughly thousand-year epochs during which, first, Shakyamuni's teachings were valid—the Early Day of the Law; second, the Middle Day of the Law, thought to correspond approximately to a period culminating in the twelfth or thirteenth century, when Shakyamuni's teachings were confused; and lastly the Latter Day of the Law, which exists up through this time, and during which people are said to be utterly confused with respect to Buddhist doctrine and are furthermore pummeled by natural and manmade disasters.

Nichiren came of age at a time during which Japan was in severe turmoil. Natural disasters, such as earthquakes and tsunamis, were ravaging the country, and Japan was invaded, unsuccessfully but alarmingly, by the Mongol Empire. Nichiren perceived his circumstances—the condition of Japan during his lifetime, the dawn of the Latter Day of the Law, and his own persecutions—as evidence that the time had come to reveal the true teaching, or one True Law, of Shakyamuni. Zhiyi had suggested such a law in his earlier writings but presumably perceived that the time of his day—the Middle Day of the Law—was not yet ripe to reveal it. Nichiren, deeply immersed in Zhiyi's treatises, and an expert in all of Shakyamuni's sutras contemporaneously available to him, concluded from these perspectives that the time to reveal any such True Law was concomitant with his advent. Based on his understanding that the title of the Lotus Sutra contained all the wisdom of its teachings, he advocated the placement of the devotional "Namu" before its title, as a prefix, and instructed his followers to chant *Nam-myoho-renge-kyo*. Nichiren explained that just as the ocean contains water from all the countless streams and rivers, the title of the Lotus Sutra, alone, is like such a drop of water, and accordingly encompasses within it all the wisdom that the Lotus Sutra reveals.

"Namu" expresses an attitude of reverence and devotion. Indeed, it appears at the beginning of most of Shakyamuni's sutras. "Myo" represents the mystery of life, which can neither be expressed in words nor even comprehended by the mind. "Ho," of myoho, indicates the manifestations of the mystical nature of life. "Renge" literally means lotus flower, and it's used to symbolize the wonder of this mystic law. The lotus flower has long been prized in Buddhism, as well as in many Asian expressions of art, for its ability to rise out of a muddy swamp yet produce beautiful, immaculate and fragrant flowers. Moreover, the blossom of the lotus, when it opens, already possesses a large number of seeds, symbolizing the simultaneity of cause and effect. Finally, "kyo" means sutra, and it indicates that our lives at each moment, whether good or evil, are inherently wondrous.

Nam-myoho-renge-kyo, referred to at times by Nichiren as the Mystic Law, and also known as daimoku (literally, "title"), is mystic because it can't logically be fathomed, but is a law because it's said to bring forth benefit and enlightenment when invoked on a daily basis and with openhearted faith. Moreover, Nichiren viewed *Myoho-renge-kyo* as identical to neither the scriptural text nor its meaning, but to the heart of the entire Lotus Sutra. In other of Nichiren's writings, the collected volumes of which are known as Gosho, he compared the nature of the daimoku to the words "India," or "Japan," which evoke all of the provinces, people and animals residing within:

> *It is like hearing someone's voice and knowing what the person must look*
> *like, or seeing someone's footprints and judging whether the person is large*
> *or small. Or it is like estimating the size of a pond by looking at the lotuses*
> *that grow in it, or imagining the size of the dragons by observing the rain*
> *that they cause to fall. Each of these examples illustrates the principle that*
> *all things are expressed in one.*

Nichiren's insight with respect to the simple mantra of *Nam-myoho-renge-kyo*, came on the heels of another larger Buddhist development in Japan: that of the Pure Land school, which encouraged the chanting of a different phrase, *Namu-amida-butsu*. This school, popular to this day in Japan but with a presence in the United States limited largely to immigrant Japanese communities, teaches that the invocation of the name of Amida Buddha would deliver one to a promised, in a sort of Judeo-Christian context, "pure land" upon death. Nichiren rejected this teaching, holding that it was both not grounded in Shakyamuni's sutras and cultivated an apathetic attitude toward life. Moreover, he argued that it was indeed possible to reach enlightenment in this life.

In Nichiren's eyes, the teachings of the Early or Middle Days of the Law, which included, in his view, all of the other Buddhist schools of his time, were no longer valid—in essence, their prescriptions had expired. The "pure land," in his view, exists only in the defiled, samsara world.

Instead, according to Nichiren, in the Latter Day of the Law, where people are so confused and defiled, a new and true Buddhist dharma must be established that would be both easy to practice and more efficient than any of the older ways. And whereas one aspect of that practice is to chant

Nam-myoho-renge-kyo, the other aspect is to direct that chanting to a mandala called a Gohonzon, or "object of devotion."

The Gohonzon

The original, "Dai-Gohonzon," of which most other extant Gohonzons are replicas, was inscribed by Nichiren in 1279 and represented the culmination of his enlightenment. The inscription of this mandala, on a lacquered, wooden board, was catalyzed by the arrest of twenty farmers, all followers of the controversial monk, who were then pressured by the governing authorities at the time to renounce their faith. None of them did, and three of the farmers, in turn, were beheaded. It is believed that Nichiren revealed this final element of his teaching in response to the courage and the depth of faith of these ordinary people. The willing execution of these farmers, who chose death before compromising their beliefs, signaled to Nichiren that the time was right to reveal this object of devotion. This original Dai-Gohonzon has been passed down through the centuries and is in the possession of the Nichiren Shoshu temple at the foot of Mount Fuji.

Each Soka Gakkai member, upon deciding to practice faith and join the organization, receives his or her smaller Gohonzon, which is a replica of the original reproduced on rice paper and enshrined within an altar in each member's home. The Gohonzon is placed in a protective box, known as a *butsudan*, which can be either ordinary or ornate, positioned at the center of the altar, and surrounded by leaves, incense, candles, and a cup of water representing, as with Zen, the various elements of the earth. The practitioner sits either on a pillow, a bench, or a chair, with legs comfortably crossed, or tucked under his or her flanks, back straight, and eyes wide open and focused on the Gohonzon. Unlike the meditation mudras, the hands of an SGI-USA member grasp a set of wooden prayer beads, with palms together and hands positioned straight and in front of the upper part of the chest. A small bell or gong is struck, and, with a strong voice and at a pace said to match the cadence of a galloping horse, the practitioner directs his or her chanting of the daimoku to the Gohonzon.

The Gohonzon is a mandala that embodies the eternal and intrinsic law of *Nam-myoho-renge-kyo*. It is meant to be a physical representation of the

Ceremony in the Air, an exquisite and poetic parable of enlightenment described by Shakyamuni in the Lotus Sutra. This ceremony depicts a "treasure tower" emerging from the earth. Shakyamuni summons all the Buddhas from all directions of the universe, stations himself in midair, opens the treasure tower and takes a seat within, beside another Buddha known as Buddha Many Treasures. Using his transcendental powers, Shakyamuni, according to the Lotus Sutra, lifts the entire assembly into the air, thus signifying his teaching's transcendence of time and space. This begins the Ceremony in the Air. At first Shakyamuni urges those in attendance to propagate the Lotus Sutra in the evil days following his death, and the innumerable bodhisattvas present agree to do so, even if they were to encounter difficult persecutions. After several discourses and chapters of the sutra, Shakyamuni ultimately transfers the essence of the sutra specifically to the gathered "Bodhisattvas of the Earth" and entrusts them with its propagation in the Latter Day of the Law. Once this transmission is accomplished, the treasure tower reverts to its former position within the earth, and the ceremony comes to an end. The heart of this allegory illustrates the revelation of Shakyamuni's original enlightenment and the transfer of the essence of this sutra to the bodhisattvas of the earth—or the masses of believers in the Latter Day of the Law.

With respect to his inscription of the Gohonzon, Nichiren wrote, "I, Nichiren, have inscribed my life in *sumi* ink,[2] so believe in the Gohonzon with your whole heart." The connotation here is that Nichiren poured the essence of his life force and enlightenment into the very ink of the characters inscribed on the Gohonzon. Thus, when chanting *Nam-myoho-renge-kyo* to the Gohonzon, a certain fusion takes place such that an individual practitioner's inherent Buddha nature is made manifest and becomes one with the enlightenment of the Buddha. From the perspective of cause and effect, it is the fundamental cause for attaining enlightenment, the seed for its attainment.

Down the center of the Gohonzon are written the Chinese characters *Nam-myoho-renge-kyo*. At the bottom of the scroll, after this inscription, are the characters for Nichiren. This is meant to underscore the oneness with the Mystic Law, and that each imperfect human being has within him or her, and can reveal the state of life of, the Buddha. On either side are characters for

---

2. A traditional Japanese ink used in art and calligraphy, which is made from the soot of pine branches and other materials.

the names of beings representing each of the Ten Worlds. At the top of the Gohonzon, the names of Shakyamuni Buddha and Buddha Many Treasures appear respectively to the immediate left and right of the inscribed daimoku. They represent the realm or world of Buddhahood. The names of four bodhisattvas who lead the other Bodhisattvas of the Earth are depicted to the left and right of the two Buddhas. They, along with the characters for other bodhisattvas depicted on the Gohonzon, represent the realm of bodhisattvas. Also depicted are the names of persons of the two vehicles—voice-hearers and cause-awakened ones, such as Shariputra and Mahakasyapa—and flanking them are representatives of the realm of heavenly beings, such as the Hindu deities Brahma and Shakra, the devil king of the sixth heaven, and the gods of the sun and moon. In the third row appears the name of a wheel-turning king, representing the realm of human beings; an *asura* king, representing the realm of angry spirits; a dragon king, representing the realm of animals; the Mother of Demon Children and her ten demon daughters, representing the realm of hungry spirits; and Devadatta, the self-declared enemy of Shakyamuni, representing the realm of hell. Characters representing the four heavenly kings are positioned in the four corners of the Gohonzon. Also depicted are the principles that earthly desires are enlightenment, and that the sufferings of birth and death are nirvana. All of these characters express the view that the Ten Worlds, as described by Zhiyi, exist within the eternal Buddha's life, and that each living being of the Ten Worlds can attain Buddhahood. The names of Zhiyi and Dengyo are inscribed in the lower part of the Gohonzon, representing those who transmitted this lineage of Buddhism. There are two inscriptions on the sides historically attributed to Zhiyi's disciple, Miao-lo, which refer to practitioners of the Lotus Sutra. One reads, "Those who vex or trouble them will have their heads split into seven pieces." The other states, "Those who give alms to them will enjoy good fortune surpassing the ten honorable titles," which are epithets applied to the Buddha expressing his virtue, wisdom, and compassion. In the lower right is Nichiren's declaration that, "This is the great mandala never before known in the entire land of Jambudvipa in the more than 2,230 years since the Buddha's passing."[3]

---

3. In Nichiren's day it was thought that Shakyamuni had passed into nirvana at about 1000 B.C. Modern scholarship variously puts Shakyamuni's passing at around the sixth century B.C.

Apart from the inscription of *Nam-myoho-renge-kyo*, most of these characters appear in an inverse fashion, as if they, along with the practitioner chanting to the Gohonzon, are facing the treasure tower on a three-dimensional plane—in other words, actually participating in the Ceremony in the Air every time a person opens the butsudan to chant.

Interestingly, most SGI-USA members might not have memorized what most of the various figures on the Gohonzon represent. In part, that's because the characters appear in classical Chinese; for another thing, the Soka Gakkai prizes experiential faith much more than esoteric study.

Rather, when a person chants the daimoku to the Gohonzon, they invariably report feelings of instant well-being. Some people, after a prolonged chanting session, say they emerge with a glowing feeling—there is a happiness that seems to spring from within. That happiness, according to SGI-USA members, is accompanied by a strong sense of confidence and courage. Some distinguish the effect of just chanting *Nam-myoho-renge-kyo* without the presence of a Gohonzon to that of chanting directly to a Gohonzon as the difference between the strumming of an acoustic guitar to that of an electric guitar with a high-volume stack of amplifiers. The Gohonzon, in this sense, is a catalyst stimulating the manifestation of one's Buddha nature. The Gohonzon is also often referred to as a mirror, much like a Tibetan Buddhist might refer to his or her teacher as a mirror. In this case, the mirror is a depiction of life organized around the central core of *Nam-myoho-renge-kyo*. When a person chants—a process that requires both faith and practice—he or she will speak of epiphanies that occur during the chanting, which often lead to instinctive insights about how they should proceed with their various life challenges. Where Zen and Tibetan Buddhists speak of a clear, placid lake, or of satori and mahamudra, Soka Gakkai Buddhists describe the achievement of similar life states through the daily practice of chanting.

The attitude that Soka Gakkai Buddhists have while chanting is unlike that of Zen or Tibetan Buddhists, and even unlike those of people of other faiths who pray. Where a Zen or Tibetan Buddhist seeks to still the mind, the Soka Gakkai Buddhist, while chanting, often reflects on his or her various prayers, reviews his or her desires, determines to win over obstacles and seldom speaks of achieving a state of detachment or bliss—although that sometimes does happen. Moreover, the prayer is not one of supplication.

SGI-USA members are encouraged not to chant as if praying to God, but rather to chant with a decided assertiveness, not unlike Nichiren when he dismounted his horse prior to his near-execution to demand support from the deity known as Hachiman.

After a while of chanting, say, perhaps an hour, the personal prayers tend to fall away and the practitioner is filled with a genuine sense of strength and well-being. At that point, SGI-USA members often say they enter a sort of powerful life state during which they chant just for the joy of chanting. It feels good to chant. And the more one does it, the better one feels. More profoundly, these are the moments when connections to the Gohonzon are palpably established—SGI-USA members call this *kyochi myogo*, or the fusion of objective reality and subjective wisdom. It is this life state, accomplished by the chanting with deep faith of *Nam-myoho-renge-kyo* to the Gohonzon, that the condition of Buddhahood becomes manifest.

SGI-USA members also perform a morning and evening liturgy, known as *gongyo*, or assiduous practice. This liturgy, which is considered to be in support of the chanting of daimoku—like salt as flavor, so to speak—consists of portions of the second ("Expedient Means") and sixteenth ("Life Span") chapters of the Lotus Sutra. As noted earlier, these chapters reinforce the notion that all people—regardless of social standing or gender—can achieve enlightenment in this lifetime, and that the Buddha's enlightenment dates from the remotest past.

In years past, the recitation of gongyo was much longer than it is today, but the SGI-USA, following its split from the Nichiren Shoshu clergy, modified the prayers so that they are more accessible to a community of busy laypersons. Where the entire recitation of the Lotus Sutra portions of the liturgy used to take close to a half hour, it now takes about five minutes, twice a day. Of course, this is meant to be followed by the chanting of *Nam-myoho-renge-kyo*, which, depending on the individual, can last anywhere from five minutes to several hours, and a concentration on various silent prayers that are performed at the opening and closing of the entire chanting session. These prayers essentially express gratitude toward *shoten zenjin*, the unseen protective forces in life believed to be activated by chanting the Mystic Law; appreciation for Nichiren and his true disciples from the thirteenth century, as well as an appreciation for Makiguchi, Toda and Ikeda as mentors; determination to transform one's suffering into benefit and for the accomplishment of personal goals; remembrance and honoring of family and friends who have passed away; and a desire for the accomplishment of peace throughout the world.

Propagating the Practice

Another element of an SGI-USA member's practice is the effort to convert friends and family to the faith. On the one hand, this missionary aspect of the Soka Gakkai stands in stark contrast to the more mellow and gradual approach to conversion embraced by the Zen and Tibetan Buddhist schools, but on the other it represents a forthright and sincere effort by practitioners to help relieve the sufferings of others—which, at its heart, is what Shakyamuni long ago held Buddhism is supposed to be about.

Efforts at conversion, known as *shakubuku*—literally, "break and subdue"—are believed to be the fastest way to change one's karma, or, as the Tibetan Buddhists put it, to develop merit. The idea is that if someone is suffering, then why not introduce him or her to the relatively easy task of chanting *Nam-myoho-renge-kyo*? There's little cost involved—joining the SGI-USA and receiving the Gohonzon requires that one spends about the same as one might for lunch. The SGI practitioner, by giving other people the opportunity to chant and become happy, performs something similar to what the Dalai Lama called "wise selfishness." Accordingly, the SGI Buddhist not only helps others to improve their lives, but makes a positive cause for his or her own by acting in an ultimately altruistic manner.

The SGI-USA has received negative media coverage over the meaning of shakubuku. For one thing, the missionary zeal of the organization was in years past considerable, rivaling at times that of network marketing ventures. People used to stand on street corners and give out literature, stop passersby to teach them how to say *Nam-myoho-renge-kyo*, and invite perfect strangers into members' homes in order to convert them to the practice. In part, the SGI-USA had proselytized in this way in order to satisfy the demands of its former, and parochial, clergy. Once the Soka Gakkai was out from under the narrow constraints of Nichiren Shoshu, however, the SGI-USA settled into a much more balanced sort of culture. Propagation is still important, but it isn't zealous. Moreover, "break and subdue" is not meant to be taken literally—SGI-USA members are not seeking to break and subdue individuals. Rather, shakubuku relates to breaking an attachment to erroneous teachings and worldly concerns, as well as distorted views of self, that cause us all to suffer. It is a term that appears in the Lotus Sutra, as well as in Zhiyi's *Great Concentration and Insight*. Nichiren, in reference to this method of spreading the teachings, relied on Bodhisattva Never Disparaging, who is described in the Lotus Sutra as bowing down to and offering appreciation to everyone he met, as an example of one who practiced shakubuku. In other words, by spreading the word of Buddhism, one seeks to sever, or break and subdue, the influence of the three poisons, negative influences, or related worldly attachments that cause each of us to suffer.

The further idea behind propagating the faith is that this is how peace will spread. The SGI-USA has no particular economic or political agenda to foist upon America. Rather, it is a very well-organized association of like-minded people chanting *Nam-myoho-renge-kyo* to (1) change their individual lives for the better, and (2) help other people to do so in order to achieve a stable society and world peace. SGI-USA members, like other Buddhists, embrace the idea of *esho funi*, or the oneness or nonduality of life and its environment. Nichiren wrote, "To illustrate, environment is like the shadow, and life, the body. Without the body, no shadow can exist, and without life, no environment. In the same way, life is shaped by its environment." According to this principle, as each individual becomes happier, then the ripples of that happiness will spread to his or her environment—family and friends. In turn, as many of them embrace faith and also become happy, those seeds of individual happiness ultimately will sprout into great orchards and be reflected in the larger society. That's the Soka Gakkai recipe for peace—it's certainly a long vision, but most, if not all, Buddhists would agree that the surest, and possibly only, road to peace is for each individual to subdue his or her delusions and become happy—one by one.

Where the dharma of Soka Gakkai Buddhism is crucially grounded in the act of chanting *Nam-myoho-renge-kyo* to the Gohonzon, study, as with Zen and Tibetan Buddhism, is also an emphasized aspect. Whereas one can study many writings relating to the Soka Gakkai, including translations and interpretations of the Lotus Sutra, or the weekly or monthly publications that the organization prepares, the primary sources of study are in two main forms. The *Writings of Nichiren Daishonin* provides one exceptional source with respect to how to practice the faith. The prolific writings of Daisaku Ikeda is the other.

Mentor and Disciple in the SGI

Although membership in the Soka Gakkai by no means requires one to consider Daisaku Ikeda as mentor, he is considered as such by the majority of Soka Gakkai members. Ikeda is, at the time of this publication, 85 years old, and while he no longer travels overseas, he remains active at the helm of the worldwide organization. SGI-USA members consider him to have inherited the true transmission of the faith from the previous two Soka Gakkai presidents, Tsunesaburo Makiguchi and Josei Toda, the latter with whom he personally studied. The mentor-student relationship in the Soka Gakkai is markedly different than that of Zen or Tibetan Buddhism, but it's no less vital. Whereas the latter schools encourage its students to choose from a variety of active mentors within their relatively immediate environments, the Soka Gakkai considers its three founding presidents—Makiguchi, Toda, and Daisaku Ikeda—as its eternal leaders or mentors. In practical terms, today's Soka Gakkai members focus on Ikeda as mentor.

This is often a difficult concept for newer SGI-USA members to accept. Why is this guy, so far away, who doesn't speak English, my mentor? How can

SGI President Daisaku Ikeda (left) with former United Nations Secretary General Boutros Boutros-Ghali, in 1993.

I establish a relationship with someone that I've never met and probably never will? These are fair questions.

While it would be thrilling to have a mentor that is constantly at one's arm, the truth is that the person, as mentor, is far less important than the teaching he or she expounds. Clearly, the sixth-century Zhiyi was a mentor to thirteenth-century Nichiren, and Shakyamuni a mentor to all of the great Buddhist founders and reformers even thousands of years after his death. On a more prosaic plane, many well known writers and artists embrace long-ago mentors to accelerate the quality of their creative works. Even elected officials, at times, consider historic political figures to be their mentors.

Because the Soka Gakkai, and more importantly, its members, views Daisaku Ikeda as the real thing—the true inheritor of the transmission of the Soka Gakkai's mission and faith—they place all their eggs, so to speak, in his basket. It's subjective, of course, but we've already seen the trap one can fall into, as with Michael Roach and Tibetan Buddhism, if a person is unfortunate enough to select the wrong mentor. Perhaps because Zen and Tibetan Buddhism places primary value on the practitioner's own experience and his or her own negotiation of the path to enlightenment, a physically present mentor is more efficacious in those schools than one who remains outside of the United States for extended periods of time. But for the SGI-USA, in which there is definitely a right and a wrong way to practice, it's apparent that the responsibility for guiding that faith needs to be centralized, of sorts, in the form of one great mentor.

The SGI, as an international organization, aims to help accomplish global peace. It wants its members to be united, "many in body, one in mind," in the words of Nichiren, and that's a tough challenge with even one mentor, let alone hundreds or thousands expressing their own differing points of view. In contrast, the respective religious practices of Zen or Tibetan Buddhism somewhat vary from monastery to monastery and sect to sect. Aside from the laudable political aspirations of Tibetans to regain control of their homeland, there's no global agenda, as in the case of the SGI, other than helping members to pursue their individual quests for enlightenment. Accordingly, there's never been a motive to consolidate the tenets of the Zen or Tibetan Buddhist faiths. But where a religious organization has a stated agenda to accomplish peace that requires a certain unified approach to matters of faith, it's both practical and efficient to have the focus be on one mentor.

From the perspective of most SGI-USA members, it is the reality of Daisaku Ikeda's achievements, far and above anyone else practicing today, that form the basis for such trust. Makiguchi stood up to Japanese militarists. Toda spread the faith throughout Japan. And Ikeda has taken it to some 180 countries worldwide. In that pursuit, he expanded the membership of the SGI movement twenty-fold. His collected speeches, rooted always in the teachings of Nichiren and the lessons he learned from his mentor, Toda, who designated the young Ikeda to be his successor, are voluminous and readily available for SGI-USA members to study.

These writings are characterized by an eclectic mix of contemporaneous thinking and ancient Buddhist wisdom. Ikeda draws on sources as diverse as American jazz music, Thai sayings, the poetry of Goethe, and myriad other cultural touchstones to demonstrate how Buddhism manifests itself in daily life—and how daily life can be illuminated further by these same Buddhist teachings. His mastery of Buddhism is matched by a palpable joy, expressed often through poetry and photographs, which permeates his work and inspires those who study it.

Numerous individuals who personally have met Ikeda over the years describe him as unfailingly considerate and sincere. He is a person, they say, who makes efforts to support others. There is no hypocrisy, no separation between what he teaches and how he acts. Cornell Capa, for one, the late brother of famed war photographer Robert Capa, who was killed in conflict, was so moved by his relationship with Ikeda that he bequeathed to him his brother's bloodstained final camera.

If nothing else, Daisaku Ikeda, as SGI president and mentor to millions, has shown enormous restraint. He has not taken advantage of the international organization for personal gain. He lives modestly. He has walked his path as both a disciple and a mentor with the understanding that no one must be sacrificed in order for the end to justify any means.

Most of all, Daisaku Ikeda is beloved by SGI-USA members to an extent that far surpasses the affection shown toward other Soka Gakkai leaders— of which there are many. It is the sangha, ultimately, that chooses, and in a sense empowers, the mentor. And it is the development of these students or disciples toward Buddhahood that determines whether or not any mentor truly is great.

PART Three

·

THE THIRD JEWEL:
THE SANGHA

·

8

Relatively Speaking:
Logic, Ethics, and Zen

The third of the Three Jewels in Buddhism is the "sangha," or the community of believers. In its traditional meaning, the sangha refers to the monks and nuns that comprise a monastic order. The very first sangha was established by Shakyamuni to provide a vehicle for those who wanted to dedicate their lives to pursuing the dharma. Over the history of Buddhism, monastic life has been considered the most suitable environment to pursue the quest for enlightenment, as the secluded monastery was seen to protect and separate the practitioner from the temptations of worldly life. Such temptations include not only sensual pleasures but also the need to earn a living, as well as the demands of family.

The sangha, in this monastic sense, has the dual role of serving the Buddhist lay community as well as preserving, and correctly transmitting to future generations, the teachings. Until the twentieth century, it was exclusively the monks of any given monastic sangha who would translate the teachings into new languages and also propagate the faith.

Up until the advent of Zen and some of the other Japanese Buddhist schools, including those based on Nichiren's teachings, monks adhered to a rigorous set of rules known as *vinaya*. These rules prescribed celibacy and strict dietary regulations for monks, as well as elaborate procedures for prayer, meditation, study, liturgy recitation, work, and begging for alms. In the thirteenth century, Japanese Buddhist leaders did away with such formalities, resulting in the rise of more secular priests or ministers, rather than cloistered monks.

Still, the monastic sangha in Zen tries, with mixed results in the United States at least, to live with as few possessions as possible. Ideally, they will retain a few black robes, a razor, a prayer cushion, some books for study, and very little else. Although not all Buddhist monks are vegetarian, Zen monks traditionally are. The food one receives at an American Zen monastery is typically quite good, simple as it may be. The preparation of a meal in the world of Zen is itself a sacred practice of mindfulness. There is no doubt that the meal itself will be delicious when it's prepared with consideration and respect. A typical monastery diet has within it many fresh vegetables, some of which more than likely were grown and harvested on the monastery grounds, and may include a variety of root vegetables, mushrooms, bamboo shoots, soy, soups, pickles, and various grains and beans. Before the meal is consumed, Zen Buddhist monks will light incense and recite a meal liturgy, known as a meal *gatha*, a grace of sorts, to express gratitude and remind themselves of their constant quest for enlightenment. The Zen Mountain Monastery's meal gatha is as follows:

First, seventy-two labors brought us this food,
We should know how it comes to us.
Second, as we receive this offering,
We should consider
Whether our virtue and practice deserve it.
Third, as we desire the natural order of mind,
To be free from clinging,
We must be free from greed.
Fourth, to support our life, we take this food.
Fifth, to attain our way we take this food.
First, this food is for the Three Treasures.
Second, it is for our teachers, parents, nation,
And all sentient beings.
Third, it is for all beings in the three worlds.
Thus, we eat this food with everyone,
We eat to stop all evil, to practice good,
To save all sentient beings,
And to accomplish our Buddha Way.

The food is eaten slowly and in silence. In this way, the preparation and digestion of the meal is itself a mindfulness practice. Such focus, at a monastery, extends to any number of other practices, including art, all forms of work, and even exercise.

Although Buddhism traditionally distinguished between the sangha—the clergy, in a traditional sense—and what was referred to as the *parisa*—the lay members—most people in the West now incorporate both communities into the meaning of sangha. Nevertheless, throughout much of Asia, monastics still teach and counsel the laity, while the lay followers offer donations in support. For many Asian Buddhists, in fact, such donations are as far as they take their practice of Buddhism. In the United States, however, and particularly in the Zen, Tibetan, and Soka Gakkai communities, it is a fully engaged laity that in many ways drives the faith.

Zen Buddhism in the United States is welcome to all people, regardless of gender, race, sexual orientation, or any other expression of identity. Buddhism recognizes a person's inherent Buddha nature. Anything else is considered a lesser self.

It's very difficult to determine how many Americans actually practice Zen Buddhism. Without doubt, hundreds of thousands at least have dabbled in it. There are currently about seventy-five Zen centers and monasteries in twenty-two states, with about a third of those located in California. The trendy notion of "zen"—the application of intense focus to a particular discipline—has certainly penetrated the American psyche and lexicon, but this is due more to popular writers than to the dissemination of any particular religious philosophy. It's probably safe to say that upwards of tens of thousands people throughout the country seriously practice Zen Buddhism. Perhaps as many as a million more have experienced it or, due to reading about and finding some resonance with the philosophy, personally consider themselves to be as much Zen as anything else.

Most Zen practitioners tend to be white—odd, on its face, for a religion imported from China and Japan. In part, this demographic is a function of the general lack of piety in Zen communities in Asia as compared to the more inspired and more recently developed American Buddhist sangha. Japanese, Korean, or Chinese immigrants to the United States, in general, could care less about practicing their native Buddhist faith. But more to the point, the costs entailed in learning how to practice Zen can be prohibitive. A monastery retreat will cost a few hundred dollars for a weekend, and there are fees as well for many training courses offered at more local or urban Zen community centers. Accordingly, the divide isn't so much based on race discrimination as it is on class. Monasteries and their live-in clerics need to be financially supported, and much of that support depends on lay practitioners who tend to be well educated and financially secure. Although open to everyone, and although a visitor to almost any monastery will invariably meet at least one or two African Americans, Zen attracts practitioners who can afford it. And, so far, they have tended to be white.

Celebrity Zen

Steve Jobs was one of the more famous Zen Buddhists in the United States. Walter Isaacson, his biographer, attributed his unprecedented business focus to the training Jobs received as a student of Zen. Jobs was serious about his Zen practice and he often attended meditation retreats at Tassajara, the very first Zen monastery in America founded by Shunryu Suzuki in central California. Isaacson noted Jobs' ability to simplify things "by zeroing in on their essence." He wasn't the nicest guy, he was a world-class control freak, but no one who uses the popular products that Apple today produces can doubt Jobs' incredible focus on simplicity. The writer Steve Silberman offers an amusing but apt description of Jobs' relationship to Zen: "Sitting zazen offered Jobs a practical technique for upgrading the motherboard in his head."

The poet and musician Leonard Cohen is so devoted to his Zen practice that in 1996 he was ordained a monk with the dharma name of Jikan, or "silent one," at the Mount Baldy Zen Center in California, where he also lived for five years. In 2009, he told the *New York Times* that Zen has helped him to stop whining and to worry less about the choices he made. "All these things have their own destiny; one has one's own destiny. The older I get, the surer I am that I'm not running the show." Or, more to the point of his Zen practice, one might look to his song *Anthem:* "Ring the bells that still can ring, forget your perfect offering. There is a crack in everything, that's how the light gets in."

One of the more captivating voices in Zen today belongs to Brad Warner, a writer, punk rocker, monster-movie maker, and Soto Zen priest. His works define an unvarnished, American "hardcore Zen," for which morality is paramount, authority is to be questioned, and the process of ultimately knowing yourself, through Zen practice, is wrenching and at times ugly. Consider his honest take on zazen:

> *Zazen isn't about blissing out or going into an alpha brain-wave trance.*
> *It's about facing who and what you really are, every single goddamn*
> *moment. And you aren't bliss, I'll tell you that right now. You're a mess.*
> *We all are. But here's the thing. That mess is itself enlightenment. You'll*
> *eventually see that the "you" that's a mess isn't really "you" at all.*

American Zen Monastics and the Monastery Culture

Some conflicting personality traits emerge from discussions with serious Zen Buddhists. For one thing, many of those who are committed to Zen express a disdain for worldly matters that borders on contempt. The world is a broken place, in their view, and there is little value to be found in the trappings of twenty-first century culture or the pursuit of a corporate career. More than a few Zen monastics are terrified by the horrors of society, yet angry and frustrated about what to do in response. Perhaps a feeling of powerlessness accompanies one who withdraws from society to the monastery. In any event, that tendency toward frustration naturally is accompanied, at times, by a proclivity to sit on the mountaintop and look down in judgment on the affairs of those in the defiled and less than spiritual world.

To them Zen, and in particular the excruciating battle with oneself through the practice of zazen, is a far more compelling and valuable way to spend one's days.

At the same time, Zen has a long history of impertinence, self-effacing sarcasm, subversion, and—some might say—masochism. Bodhidharma, the patriarch, once sat in a cave for nine years to demonstrate his mastery. Legend, again hopefully apocryphal, holds that he didn't move for so long that his legs thereafter had to be amputated because they were gangrenous. Another more literal story, concerning a twentieth-century monk named Morinaga Soko, relates that he spent three winter days huddled beneath the stairs of the entrance to a Japanese monastery to demonstrate his determination to become a Zen acolyte. He was exposed to cold wind and snow and subject to verbal assaults and physical beatings. With his legs numb and his face bloody, he finally convinced the monks to take him in as a student. Zen is a practice that requires courage and determination at the outset. Gaining admission to Zen is a far cry, for example, from the Soka Gakkai's relative sign-right-here approach.

Often clerics are accused of being haughty or authoritarian, but that's the nature of the practice. In Zen, you're not supposed to necessarily love your mentor. Zen literature, as previously shown, is replete with stories of mentors shocking their students out of their stupors, sometimes through apparently inconsiderate or even violent means, but with an eye toward pointing them toward enlightenment. The problems arise when a compassionate attitude does not underlie the aggressive acts. In America, most of these Zen transgressions have been of a sexual nature.

In the early 1980s, Richard Baker, then the abbot of the San Francisco Zen Center, was persuaded to step down from his position after revelations of his relationships with various female students became public. Similar charges were leveled against Eido Shimano, a leader of the Zen Studies Society in New York, and he resigned as abbot from the organization in 2010. Another series of sexual-affair-related complaints against a Zen abbot, Dennis Genpo Merzel, led to the closing of his temple in Maine in 1990, as well as his resignation and disrobing in 2011 as the founder and abbot of a Zen center in Salt Lake City, Utah. Other Zen controversies in the United States have concerned accusations of corruption or embezzlement by clerics.

Most recently, as reported by the *New York Times* in 2013, several Zen students accused Zen master Joshu Sasaki of many instances of sexual harassment. An early and influential Japanese teacher of Zen in the United States, Sasaki, one hundred and five years old at the time of this writing, was blamed, among other things, for inappropriately touching women over many years and even asking female students to expose their breasts as a recommended method of answering koans. Still, some of his former students defended him, noting that, unwelcome sexual gestures aside, he was nevertheless an inspiring figure.

Celibacy is not a requirement for Zen priests, but the issue of masters in positions of great authority sexually preying on their students should be.

Monks sound a meditation gong at Tassajara Zen Monastery in California, the first Zen monastery established in the United States.

Yet students within the Zen sangha may not always feel free to speak out. According to Zen Master Sheng-yen, who trained himself in zazen on a Taiwanese mountaintop for more than six years of seclusion, and who passed away in 2009, "It should be remembered that the mind of the master is ever pure . . . and even if the master tells lies, steals, and chases women . . . he is still to be considered a true master as long as he scolds his disciples for their transgressions."[4] In other words, it's traditionally held that the Zen master ought to be considered infallible and omniscient, with behavior that is far beyond the capacity of his students to comprehend. His authority, legitimatized through the ritual of dharma transmission, or the affirmation of a student's enlightenment by his or her teacher, is unquestioned.

The authority of the Zen master is also underscored by dokusan in the interview room, a procedure much loved by devout Zen students. These are opportunities for individual meetings, or spiritual guidance sessions, between a mentor and his or her student. The student will enter the interview room,

---

4. Master Sheng-yen's comments were reported by the Zen scholar Stuart Lachs in a 1999 presentation to the American Academy of Religion, and were retrieved from http://terebess.hu/english/lachs.html#7.

where he will proceed to bow and prostrate himself before the master, who sits, with incense burning, before the student. The student will present whatever question he may have, or perhaps an insight gleaned from contemplation of a koan, and the master will choose to respond or not. The session is over when the master tinkles a bell. The student again bows and makes his way out of the room; the next student on the line follows and falls to his knees. This ritual is seen as critical to the study of Zen.

Morality in Zen—a practice that, at least until it arrived and was redefined in the United States, rejects at its essence both logic and ethics—is one of the six *paramitas* that Zen practitioners are instructed to uphold: charity, moral discipline, patience, diligence, meditation, and wisdom. In the Zen tradition, there is also an admonition, as one of the Ten Precepts, to not talk about the faults of others. Rather, Zen practitioners are encouraged to unconditionally accept what each moment has to offer.

So who, in particular, is drawn to the practice of Zen? Master Sheng-yen, for one, observed that many Westerners with strong egos are drawn to Zen practice, although such people also have a strong spiritual desire to confront their selfishness and self-regard. Zen is not for people with psychological disorders who would not necessarily benefit from extreme confrontations with the mind and ego. From a medical perspective, meditation has been shown to cause the brain to release serotonin. That, for almost all people, will induce feelings of relaxation and well-being, but for others it can provoke psychotic episodes.

As seen, it's not easy to join a Zen community. Certainly, it's no problem to attend a lecture or a weekend introductory seminar, but that's a far cry from cowering under a staircase for three days while being vilified and beaten. Getting serious about Zen in the United States is somewhere between these two extremes.

For one thing, Zen monasteries aren't always so easy to reach. Many are located in very rural areas. But even if one is near a Zen center, it's not always the most welcoming of environments. People are invariably nice, but unless it's an introductory workshop a person might find him- or herself feeling a bit left out. A commitment to want to learn can be demonstrated by helping out at the monastery or the center—considerable value in the Zen community is placed on hard work and pitching in. So if a prospective student is motivated to brush off or straighten the cushions, or perhaps sweep the floor—an important aspect of monastery life, in particular—then he'll soon make a friend who will help guide him into the fold. Or simply ask if any help is needed. For sure, people with such helpful natures will find themselves with a broom or be escorted into the kitchen.

As noted, many Zen Buddhists in the United States are struggling to consider what's essentially Zen, and what is Zen's cultural baggage from Japan. This is an issue, as well, for Tibetan Buddhists and the Soka Gakkai in America. As Zen was transmitted from China to Korea and Japan, of course, it changed and adapted to fit the respective culture. It's only relatively recently arrived in the United States. Accordingly, how will it continue to evolve or transform itself to better reflect the needs of its American students?

The question of ordination, or of the clergy in general, for one, was resolved in a radical way by the Nichiren Shoshu and Soka Gakkai—the priests simply excommunicated the seventeen million lay members who no longer recognized their pretense to unquestioned authority, but how might that model apply to Zen? With the advent of profoundly experienced Zen students who are not clerics, are priests even necessary?

There is, of course, a general understanding in the Zen community that teachers, quite apart from monks, are absolutely vital. And that the requirements to becoming a teacher—the years of practice, the dharma transmission from a trusted senior master—are still effective methods to ensure that good teachers continue to be produced. In this respect, there appears in Zen to be very little of the sort of tension between the laity and the monastics as became manifest in the Nichiren Shoshu–Soka Gakkai dispute.

Of greater interest to Zen practitioners in the United States is the distinctly American desire for diversity. Although Zen has had relatively poor results, so far, in attracting nonwhite students, it has had some terrific appeal in the gay community. Several local LGBT Zen groups and sanghas can be found in major cities across the country. In this context, one of the more intriguing figures in American Zen was Issen Dorsey, a gay Zen teacher and priest who provided devoted service to people suffering from AIDS in San Francisco during the first, terrible years of the epidemic. The Greyston Foundation, a large nonsectarian social services network in Yonkers, New York, founded by the pioneering Zen Roshi Bernie Glassman, maintains an AIDS Center, as well as a housing complex for people with HIV/AIDS. It's called Issen House, after Issen Dorsey, who himself died of the disease in 1987.

The Zen Mountain Monastery also sponsors the National Buddhist Prison Sangha (NBPS), a nationwide network of Zen Buddhist volunteers who correspond with inmates and visit prisons to create Buddhist practice groups. The group's activities include weekly visits to prisons by senior Zen students who lead zazen and give dharma lectures, periodic intensive meditation retreats at the prisons, and the performance of various ceremonies, including weddings and memorial services.

There also exists a Buddhist Military Sangha to support the reported three thousand Buddhists serving today in the U.S. armed services, including chaplains, a figure that seems to be conservative. The teachings of Buddhism, of course, are nonviolent, yet there have always been Buddhist soldiers, warriors, and defenders of nations. Moreover, while Buddhism historically nowhere near approaches the levels of war in the names of the monotheistic faiths, there have been plenty of episodes throughout history of Buddhist violence. Most conspicuous, of course, is the career of Ashoka, the ancient king of India, who was considered one of history's greatest patrons of Buddhism following his conversion to the faith after massacring many thousands of people. And during World War II, many of the soldiers of the illustrious Japanese-American 442nd infantry were Buddhist—not to mention, on the other side, members of Japan's military and its kamikaze force. The U.S. Air Force Academy maintains in its Protestant Chapel the Vast Refuge Dharma Hall Chapel, which was donated by Friends of Zen and the Frederick P. Lenz Foundation for American Buddhism, which is the first space on an American military base dedicated solely to meditation. According to *Tricycle* magazine, which covers Buddhist news and events, the Reverend Dai En Wiley Burch of the Hollow Bones Rinzai Zen school, and a graduate of the Academy, dedicated the chapel with the following words: "Without compassion, war is a criminal activity. Sometimes it is necessary to take life, but we never take life for granted."

Relativism and Absolutism

So does Buddhism, and Zen in particular, condone violence or not? More to the point, is Zen a changeable, relativist faith lacking absolute ethical positions?

Were such socially engaged American Buddhists as Robert Aitken and Bernie Glassman inspired by Zen to do good, or are they rather the sorts of people who would have been driven to help others without regard to whatever religious practice they chose to embrace?

Relativism is the intellectual ability to view the criteria of judgment to be relative, one that varies with individuals and their environments. It's a doctrine that holds no belief to be absolutely true but entirely dependent on context and circumstance. A simple, current example would involve the use of terrorism for political means. The absolutist and predominant view is that the attacks on 9/11 were heinous and reprehensible. A relativist view is that the causes underlying such terrorism, including poverty, as well as political, cultural, and religious imperialism, are apparent and egregious, and so the perpetrators of 9/11 were acting as justifiable, albeit violent, freedom fighters.

Everyone, to some extent, is relativist. We all recognize that people view the same circumstances differently, that subjectivity is a part of what most individuals would call reality.

In the case of Zen, perhaps what some people call relativist is actually counterintuitive. What Zen rejects is logical reasoning and rationality, in the tradition of the ancient Greek philosophers through to, and following, René Descartes. Nevertheless, Zen is rarely dogmatic in a traditional religious sense, and it hasn't been responsible for the sorts of atrocities historically relating to monotheistic faiths. After all, Buddhism encourages individuals to analyze issues carefully for themselves and to weigh the consequences of their actions in light of their faith and practice. Zen, particularly in America, is a liberal community in that sense—there are no moral absolutes and not a lot of telling people what to do. In Japan, though, the picture wasn't always quite as pretty.

In 1993 the Berkeley scholar Robert H. Sharf published a paper titled *The Zen of Japanese Nationalism*, which revealed the parochial and nationalist leanings of early Zen proponents in America, including D.T. Suzuki and his teacher Soen Shaku. And in 1997, the professor and Zen practitioner Brian Daizen Victoria published the book *Zen At War*. This work detailed the cooperation between Zen Buddhism and Japanese militarism from the mid-1800s through World War II, and it demonstrated that Zen provided not only a philosophical underpinning to the war effort but also active support. Although the quality of Victoria's research has been called into some question by various scholars, his publication of the book nevertheless blew a secretive lid off of the Zen community. He followed up this work with a similarly explosive look at Zen, called *Zen War Stories*.

In particular, the statements and actions of Yasutani Haku'un Roshi included in Victoria's works had a significant impact on the American Zen community. Yasutani, who first visited the United States in 1962, taught many of the pioneering American Zen leaders, including Robert Aitken and Philip Kapleau, the latter of whom published *Three Pillars of Zen*—a seminal work in the English language on Zen that prominently features Yasutani's teachings.

Zen War Stories reports that in a 1943 book published in Japan, Yasutani, who was 58 years old at the time, strongly supported the Japanese war effort and interpreted Zen teachings to deify the emperor. Moreover, he indulged in anti-Semitic statements. Among Yasutani's published thoughts:

Annihilating the treachery of the United States and Britain and establishing the Greater East Asia Co-Prosperity Sphere is the only way to save the one billion people of Asia so that they can, with peace of mind, proceed on their respective paths.

And:

What should the attitude of disciples of the Buddha, as Mahayana Bodhisattvas, be toward the first precept that forbids the taking of life? . . . Those who understand the spirit of the Mahayana precepts should be able to answer this question immediately. That is to say, of course one should kill, killing as many as possible. One should, fighting hard, kill everyone in the enemy army.

And, finally:

We must be aware of the existence of the demonic teachings of the Jews who assert things like equality in the phenomenal world, thereby disturbing public order in our nation's society and destroying governmental control.

Yasutani was accepted in the West as a considerate and humanistic teacher. His students, several of whom were Jewish, of course had no inkling of his writings during World War II, and so they were shocked by Victoria's revelations. The American Zen leaders who had studied with and knew Yasutani, who by then had passed away, denounced him for these positions, but also carved out a place for an appreciation of his teachings. In essence, they recommended a treasuring of Yasutani's teachings but not Yasutani's politics or his views as an individual. And they cautioned that the nature of his comments during the war had to be considered within the context of his times. This sort of remarkably relativist viewpoint is encountered time after time within the American Zen sangha—not only in Yasutani's defense, but also, as described earlier, in the cases of sexual indiscretions by Zen masters such as Joshu Sasaki.

Zen, which, again appears to have traditionally rejected logic and devalued rationality, provides no institutionalized system of morality for its practitioners. If anything, ethical dilemmas are left to each person to sort out based on his or her own interpretation of the Ten Precepts or the paramita with respect to moral discipline. It's inherently a faith divorced from ethical context. It's true that the Buddha taught that all people possess a Buddha nature within them, and presumably this applies to warmongers, anti-Semites, and sexual predators as well. But can an anti-Semite claim to have achieved a state of enlightenment? Can a warmonger have profound compassion for other living beings?

In Zen, the answer seems to be yes. The main thing that has mattered to Zen traditionally—outside of the United States—is the inner life, the quest for individual enlightenment. Historically, Zen otherwise seeks to be a blank slate, or a placid lake if you will, reflecting only what is projected on it—a convenient, dangerous, and vulnerable position for any philosophical system, which is what Zen surely is whether or not it pretends otherwise. Zen suggests that a sense of true morality will, like compassion, emanate naturally from the person who succeeds in achieving satori. Accordingly, if an ethical life inherently springs from one's enlightened Buddha nature—which itself, says Zen, is accessed only after profound meditation and a shattering of the way one has been trained to think—why is it that an acclaimed Zen master like Yasutani, the headwater in many respects of American Zen, could not, at a mature age, come to grips with what was right and wrong?

Yasutani's position during World War II was consistent with the nationalist sentiments of his senior Zen teachers, men like Soen Shaku and others who sought to redefine Zen and ally it with the very definition of what it meant to be Japanese in the years following the mid-nineteenth-century Meiji Restoration. When Yasutani was in Japan, he, like all other Zen adherents, reflected the prevailing social sentiments of his time. Similarly, when he taught in 1960s America, he mirrored, perhaps even without intentional calculation, the cultural mores of that place and that time.

American Zen leaders, people of rectitude and unquestionable accomplishment like Bernie Glassman or the dharma heirs of John Daido Loori, have redefined Zen in the United States and infused it with a moral compass that it appears to inherently lack. Specifically, they, along with a newer generation of Zen writers like Brad Warner, are recalibrating this ancient practice with a distinctively Western ethical touch. In doing so, they surely recognize that at least a hint of logic and moral absolutism can sometimes go a long way.

9

Tibetan Checks and Balances:
Lean in the Direction of the Dharma

The parched forests around Boulder, Colorado, burned throughout the summer of 2012, so much so that by day thick smoke obscured the view of the nearby Rocky Mountains and by night the moon rose red and orange, like fire, in starless skies.

Boulder is ground zero for Tibetan Buddhism in the United States. Marpa House, the only Buddhist layperson's residence in the country, is located there, and a rural mountain retreat, Phuntsok Choling, in nearby Ward, Colorado, offers local Buddhists frequent opportunities for meditation, contemplation, and study with leading lamas like Dzigar Kongtrul Rinpoche. The tiny campus of Naropa University also lays tucked away in Boulder, off Arapahoe Boulevard, but if you drive too fast you might miss it, surrounded as it is by the sprawling, dominating campus of the University of Colorado at Boulder.

It's close to forty years now since Naropa was founded by Chogyam Trungpa Rinpoche, almost halfway to the hundred-year project he envisioned back in 1974. In those days he had brought together an unusual and eclectic mix of Beats and Buddhists, Allen Ginsburg among them, in an endeavor to express Buddhism through a liberal arts education, without artistic fear.

That eclecticism and freedom to create is nurtured in today's Naropa University, and it's expressed, very genuinely, by the students enrolled in the school's religious studies, psychology, peace studies, writing, and other arts programs. It's an open campus, and its students are friendly, approachable, and appear genuinely happy to be there. The word everyone at Naropa, whether Buddhist or not, uses to describe the school is "contemplative." Students are there, in this Buddhist-inspired university, not only to think but to personally transform themselves.

John Cobb, the past president of Naropa, speaks of a "razor's edge" to maintain such a Buddhist inspiration within the confines of a nonsectarian institution. Naropa has no information with respect to how many Tibetan Buddhists are enrolled in its programs, but it's a safe bet that they're less than half, if that, of the student body. So it's a tightrope walk into a future without diluting Trungpa Rinpoche's original vision. Naropa challenges its students to speak up, to express themselves however uniquely, and to take the lessons learned at the school and apply them toward the creation of a more enlightened society. In Cobb's words, "there's no back row at Naropa."

As with Zen, and across the spectrum of Tibetan Buddhism in general, Naropa's student body is predominantly white with a measure of African Americans and Hispanics as well. Also like Zen, this is in no way due to any racial prohibitions but, again, it's a question of economic class. The practice of Tibetan Buddhism requires a huge investment of time and money. Accordingly, it's a faith that naturally appeals most to those in more comfortable economic situations—those with the leisure time to invest. Trungpa Rinpoche's son, Sakyong Mipham Rinpoche, has made strides to simplify certain practices, particularly through Shambhala, but the lack of ethnic balance in the Tibetan Buddhist community in America in general continues to be of concern to its institutional leaders. And it's of particular concern in Naropa, because the nature of a university—particularly this university, with its universal message and mission—requires diversity in thought, social class, experience, and custom.

Naropa's Jack Kerouac School of Disembodied Poetics is particularly renowned, as is its related Summer Writing Program, a four-week intensive training experience for students, poets, scholars, writers, Buddhist teachers, performance artists, and musicians. Students engage there in wildly experimental and lively avant-garde postmodernist writing disciplines in a self-proclaimed "Outrider" lineage—a heritage of scholarship and counter-poetics operating outside the normative academic mainstream.

In other words, this is a celebratory and soulful writing program, unlike any other academic experience, and one with a fascination not only with words and language but on how movement, Buddhism, spiritual freedom, and self-contemplation pour into the flowering of written expression.

A student writer, for example, is not simply writing at Naropa but perhaps attending at the school's intimate Performing Arts Center a Dharma Arts class focused on "embodied awareness" through dance. There are no pens, papers, or laptops at this class. Rather, the writers seek to mingle dance with meditative, mindful practices toward the aim of establishing movement awareness—an awareness of self and space around the room. A sort of mingling of 1960s experimental dance with the dharma as taught by Trungpa Rinpoche, the writers learn to be alone and to be together, to exchange gestures and to become interdependent through play. They explore the abodes of human existence—standing, walking, sitting, and lying down. At the end they find stillness and receive the energy of their fellow participants. The two hours of such exercises, it is said, instills a body-mind approach to the writing process, rather than a simple mind-driven creative impulse.

In the evenings, the Summer Writing Program is host to an impressive array of writing and art celebrities. For close to forty years, each summer has hosted a hall of fame roster of Buddhists, poets and writers, including William Burroughs, Gregory Corso, Amiri Baraka, and Gary Snyder. The 2012 program featured Anne Waldman, Thurston Moore, and Laurie Anderson, among others.

During the programs, Waldman, a pioneer Tibetan Buddhist who studied directly with Trungpa Rinpoche and helped found the Jack Kerouac School, offered a selection of muscular poetry set to music composed and presented by her son, Ambrose Bye. The Performing Arts Center was packed, and the performance of Waldman, a rock star among poets, evoked thoughts of what Jim Morrison

The Lincoln Building of Naropa University, in Boulder, Colorado, which serves as a gallery and administrative offices.

of "The Doors," might be doing today if he hadn't drowned in 1971 in that
Paris bathtub. For Waldman, Buddhism is poetry, and poetry is liberty. The
spiritual freedom of her Tibetan Buddhist faith—unconventional, fearless—
was expressed not so much by her words, which soared, but by the strong force
of her life bubbling below them.

Thurston Moore, the literal rock star on the program, wasn't nearly as
impressive. The songwriter, singer, and guitarist from "Sonic Youth" read, in
a soft, desultory voice, a sort of stream-of-consciousness liturgy about what
a drag being a protopunk god can be. Still, his solo electric guitar-feedback
performance at the end of his presentation was well worth the free price of
admission.

The playful, morbid, and very funny Laurie Anderson, Tibetan
Buddhist, performance artist, and structuralist filmmaker, recited provocative
and, at times, pretty poetry that wasn't necessarily spiritual in a Buddhist sense.
But the audience, as with most Buddhist groups, was unfailingly enthusiastic
toward Anderson and each performer, lavishing them with extended ovations,
reveling in the presence of their celebrity Buddhist brothers and sisters.

Celebrity Tibetan Buddhists

With the possible exception of the Soka Gakkai, Tibetan Buddhism in America
has drawn to it more famous practitioners than any other school of Buddhism.
Most prominently, these include Richard Gere, Steven Seagal, the composer
Philip Glass, and the actress Sharon Stone—although Stone's grasp of the faith
based on her comments to the Associated Press following the devastating 2008
earthquake in China appears to be elementary:

> I'm not happy about the way the Chinese are treating the Tibetans because
> I don't think anyone should be unkind to anyone else. . . . And then this
> earthquake and all this stuff happened, and then I thought, is that karma?
> When you're not nice that the bad things happen to you?

Gere, on the other hand, is seriously devoted to Buddhism and the Dalai
Lama and has been for many years. He first practiced Zen in his early twenties,
and then converted to Tibetan Buddhism several years later upon meeting

the Dalai Lama, whom he considers his "root guru." As told to the Buddhist magazine, *Shambhala Sun*, he has an intriguing and humble perspective on his celebrity career and his faith:

> *If I weren't out in the marketplace, there's no way I would be able to really face the nooks and crannies and darkness inside of me. I just wouldn't see it. I'm not that tough; I'm not that smart. I need life telling me who I am, showing me my mind constantly. I wouldn't see it in a cave. The problem with me is I would probably just find some blissful state, if I could, and stay there. That would be death. I don't want that. As I said, I'm not an extraordinary practitioner. I know pretty much who I am. It's good for me to be in the world.*

Seagal, the martial arts expert and film star, may be an even more fascinating Tibetan Buddhist figure. For one thing, he was recognized in 1997 by his teacher, Penor Rinpoche, as a reincarnation of a seventeenth-century figure known as Treasure Revealer Chungdrag Dorje. In the parlance of Tibetan Buddhism, therefore, Seagal is a *tulku*, or a reincarnation of a past Buddhist master. Such tulkus are said to manifest their compassion for the suffering of people, and so they vow to be reborn to help all others attain enlightenment. In defense of this recognition of Seagal's tulku status, Penor Rinpoche clarified:

> *As for Steven Seagal's movie career, my concern is with the qualities I experienced within him which relate to his potential for benefiting others and not with the conventional details of his life which are wholly secondary. Some people think that because Steven Seagal is always acting in violent movies, how can he be a true Buddhist? Such movies are for temporary entertainment and do not relate to what is real and important. It is the view of the Great Vehicle of Buddhism that compassionate beings take rebirth in all walks of life to help others. Any life condition can be used to serve beings and thus, from this point of view, it is possible to be both a popular movie star and a tulku.*

As for Seagal's take on his tulku status, his attitude, as reflected in an interview with the screenwriter Stanley Weiser, is consistent with that of a humble, practicing Buddhist: "I don't believe it is very important who I was in my last lives, I think it is important who I am in this life. And what I do in this life is only important if I can ease the suffering of others, if I can somehow make the world a better place, if I somehow serve Buddha and mankind, if I can somehow plant the seed of bodhicitta in people's hearts." Seagal, like other serious Tibetan Buddhists, also revealed that he practices guru yoga, prostrations, and other secret meditation methods assigned to him by his teachers. "I am not a highly realized being, I am not a great lama, I don't have any great practice. I am a very low person just trying to get to first base and the most basic practice of a bodhisattva. I am starting humble memorizations, meditations, and prayers."[5]

Interestingly, Penor Rinpoche, the highly honored eleventh throne holder of the Palyul Lineage of the Nyingma school, also recognized the first Western woman, Jetsunma Ahkon Lhamo, as a tulku. Jetsunma, originally from Canarsie, Brooklyn, was before her tulku recognition known for her psychic abilities, channeling beings called Santu and Andor, as well as the prophet Jeremiah. Since the mid-1980s, she and her Tibetan Buddhist followers in Maryland have held continuous twenty-four-hour prayer vigils dedicated to the end of all suffering.

A Difficult Birth

In some respects, the American Tibetan Buddhist community got off to a very rough start. Trungpa Rinpoche, and his crazy wisdom in the 1970s and early 1980s, at best challenged and at worst alienated his first American followers. Pema Chodron, the respected Vajrayana nun and popular writer, was, and remains, a devoted disciple of Trungpa Rinpoche and yet acknowledges his drinking, his sexual liaisons with other female students, his tendency toward chaos, and his frequent needling. Yet such provocations, Chodron believes, were deliberate and meant to help others, to shake the foundations of comfort and habitual patterns, which, to Trungpa Rinpoche, were no more than false and delusional securities. At that time, the single-minded devotion to the teacher would border on the ridiculous. When he smoked, members of his sangha started to smoke. When he would stop, they would. Still, many of his disciples maintain that Trungpa Rinpoche's motivation,

---

5. The full interview with Seagal is published at http://www.elevenshadows.com/tibet/seagalinterview1.htm.

in every respect, was to help people by shaking them up. Of course, not everyone on the receiving end of insults or sexual harassment agreed.

Children of those pioneer American Tibetan Buddhists recall attending magical Black Crown Ceremonies, in which the Karmapa, the head of the Kagyu lineage, would place a black crown on his head and radiate such compassion that it would reportedly fly away if he didn't hold on to it tightly. They would enroll in Shambhala Sun summer camps, in the mountains near Boulder, to practice meditation, awareness training, and military forms of British drill. The goals were to learn how to focus one's mind and to apply discipline toward bringing forth gentleness and sincerity.

Undoubtedly the nadir of the U.S. experience in Tibetan Buddhism occurred following Trungpa Rinpoche's 1986 death. Shortly thereafter, it was revealed that his dharma heir, Osel Tendzin, a Passaic, New Jersey, native and the first Western lineage holder in the Kagyu and Nyingma traditions, had contracted HIV. Not only that, but the Vajra Regent, as he was called, had known this for nearly three years yet continued to have unprotected sex with his male and female students without informing them. At least one of those students reportedly later died of AIDS. Tendzin himself passed away from the disease in 1990. The scandal, as one would expect, ripped the sangha apart.

From there, somehow, the sangha began to heal, and today it is arguably among the strongest Buddhist communities in America. The Dalai Lama, surely, has played a significant role in its recovery.

Aside from the Shambhala centers spread throughout the country, the Nobel Prize-winning Dalai Lama and his writings remain the primary touchstones for Americans interested in Tibetan Buddhism. He is described by those who have met him as, among other things, considerate, amusing, open, profound, humble, intelligent, sweet, strict, joyful, and glowing.

The Dalai Lama first visited America in 1979, when he spoke to fairly small crowds at Seattle University and the University of Washington. By 1987, his world renown had grown to the extent that he addressed the United States Congress and proposed his "Five Point Peace Plan." This Plan, among other propositions, called for a transfer of the entire nation of Tibet into a zone of peace and for the abandonment of China's population transfer policy through which the indigenous Tibetans are becoming culturally and economically overwhelmed by the state-sponsored influx of Chinese immigrants.

In 1989 he received the Nobel Prize for Peace. In his acceptance speech, he noted that the prior week saw several Tibetans sentenced to terms of up to nineteen years in prison for expressing their desire to see the restoration of Tibet's independence. "As a Buddhist monk, my concern extends to all members of the human family and, indeed, to all sentient beings who suffer. I believe all suffering is caused by ignorance. People inflict pain on others in the selfish pursuit of their happiness or satisfaction. Yet true happiness comes from a sense of brotherhood and sisterhood. We need to cultivate a universal responsibility for one another and the planet we share."

In 2007, the Dalai Lama received the Congressional Gold Medal, the highest civilian award bestowed by the U.S. Congress, in an event that was broadcast live to Tibetans worldwide. By then his smiling, benevolent image had been impressed upon most Americans. But what of his fellow six million Tibetans and their fate?

The Politics of Tibet

The Dalai Lama, of course, is himself a refugee, having fled Tibet ten years after China's first invasion in 1949. According to some Tibetan sources, as many as 250,000 Tibetans have since died in prison. Nuns have been brutalized by torture. Women have been raped, sterilized, and forced to have abortions. At one point, during Mao Zedong's "Great Leap Forward," all but six out of 6,000 Tibetan Buddhist monasteries reportedly were destroyed. What has happened to Tibet over the past sixty years is nothing short of an ethnic and religious cleansing. In his speech to the United States Congress in 1987, the Dalai Lama called it a "holocaust."

Patience in Tibet has run thin, and monks there have become uncharacteristically politicized. Since 2009, in a phenomenon that continues to grow, dozens of young Tibetans—monks and laypersons—have protested their utter lack of freedoms and the destruction of their language, religion, and culture through self-immolations, resulting in death to most of the individual protestors. It's been called the largest-ever group of self-immolation protests for one cause in history, and it of course brings into sharp question Buddhism's uncompromising demand for nonviolence. According to Human Rights Watch, China has responded, in part, by cutting off all news in Tibet through restrictions on Internet usage, text messaging, phone ownership, music publishing, and photocopying.

Political motives aside, Buddhism generally would consider harming oneself to be a violent act, although, in the Dalai Lama's view, it appears that the motivation for the act, rather than the act itself, is what determines its value. In November 2012 he told Ann Curry of the *Today* show:

> *Whether this kind of method is right or wrong is difficult to judge. . . . They're in a desperate situation. They take these decisions. I'm quite certain those cases who sacrifice their own life for sincere motivation, for Buddha dharma, for well-being of the people, from the Buddhist viewpoint, from religious viewpoint, it's positive. If carried out in full anger and hatred, then it's wrong. So it's difficult to judge. But it's very, very sad.*

Other Tibetans have taken up the cause in the United States. Shingza Rinpoche, for one, fasted with two of his fellow monks outside of the United Nations for thirty days to bring attention to the struggles of the Tibetan people. In a message he released on the fifty-third anniversary of the March 10, 1959, Tibetan uprising, he suggested that a "free and independent Tibet" was the "one and the only path" left for Tibetans. "In Tibet the brave Tibetan heroes sacrifice their lives by setting themselves on fire as an ultimate form of peaceful protest. These are clear indications for those of us living in exile to stand up and be active in our struggle for freedom more than ever before."

So the land of Tibet and its Buddhism, much like Israel and Judaism, is intertwined. And regrettably, the Tibetan faith and its people also have suffered their genocide, their diaspora, their martyrs, and a longing for a return to their Zion. A growing American sangha watches it all, expressing solidarity and empathy, but not quite sure how to help. For the most part they focus on the practice of their faith.

The Sangha as a Dharma Island

What constitutes a sangha for a Buddhist denomination split into four major schools, along with the Shambhala tradition and its more mellow approach to Vajrayana practice? In the view of Barbara Dilley, the former dancer and Naropa University president, the sangha "is a group of people facing the same direction and not leaning on one another. I think that not leaning on each other means something about not being co-dependent. This definition creates a big field holding many different folks with separate unique experiences yet together in the direction they face."

Notably, in the *Today* show interview, the Dalai Lama referred to himself as a "free spokesman" for the Tibetan people, and to the Tibetan people, themselves, as his "boss." In this context, Tibetan Buddhism, more than any other Buddhist school, places considerable influence in the hands of its followers as a triangular check-and-balance, of sorts, on its monastic leaders and their interpretations of the dharma. Indeed, the Vietnamese Zen master Thich Nhat Hanh famously said, "The next Buddha may be the Sangha itself." Does this mean that a sort of collective awakening will deliver Buddhism to a new era of enlightenment? Is it the people, ultimately, and not the teaching or the teachers who are destined to lead the way toward a new age of liberation and peace?

What even constitutes a sangha in Tibetan Buddhism? Traditionally it refers only to monastics, but that definition is irrelevant in the West. Is it every practitioner, ranging from those imprisoned in Tibet to someone enrolled at an introductory meditation class at a Shambhala center in Boulder? Does it include all the professors and students at Naropa University who may not even practice Buddhism? Or is it each individual community of believers, centered on whichever master they practice with? Does every Tibetan Buddhist, as in Dilley's perspective, face the same direction? If so, what direction might that be?

Shakyamuni, near the end of his life, spoke to his long-time attendant and close disciple, the Venerable Ananda, on this very subject. As recited in the Maha-parinibbana Sutta, a Theravada-Pali version of the Nirvana Sutra, the "community of *bhikkus*," or the sangha, should after Shakyamuni's death seek only the *dhamma* (the dharma) and not any leader who pretends to know some secret truth.[6] The Tathagata refers to Shakyamuni Buddha himself:

---

6.   This version of the Nirvana Sutra derives from the Theravada "Pali Canon." It is a fascinating, intimate, and somewhat biographical account of Shakyamuni Buddha's last days. In contrast, the several Mahayana versions of the Nirvana Sutra concern not so much the story of the end of Shakyamuni's life but his teachings on eternal true self and Buddha nature.

Then the Venerable Ananda approached the Blessed One, respectfully greeted him, and sitting down at one side, he spoke to the Blessed One, saying: "Fortunate it is for me, O Lord, to see the Blessed One at ease again! Fortunate it is for me, O Lord, to see the Blessed One recovered! For truly, Lord, when I saw the Blessed One's sickness it was as though my own body became weak as a creeper, every thing around became dim to me, and my senses failed me. Yet, Lord, I still had some little comfort in the thought that the Blessed One would not come to his final passing away until he had given some last instructions respecting the community of bhikkhus."

Thus spoke the Venerable Ananda, but the Blessed One answered him, saying: "What more does the community of bhikkhus expect from me, Ananda? I have set forth the Dhamma without making any distinction of esoteric and exoteric doctrine; there is nothing, Ananda, with regard to the teachings that the Tathagata holds to the last with the closed fist of a teacher who keeps some things back. Whosoever may think that it is he who should lead the community of bhikkhus, or that the community depends upon him, it is such a one that would have to give last instructions respecting them. But, Ananda, the Tathagata has no such idea as that it is he who should lead the community of bhikkhus, or that the community depends upon him. So what instructions should he have to give respecting the community of bhikkhus?

" . . . Therefore, Ananda, be islands unto yourselves, refuges unto yourselves, seeking no external refuge; with the Dhamma as your island, the Dhamma as your refuge, seeking no other refuge.

"And how, Ananda, is a bhikkhu an island unto himself, a refuge unto himself, seeking no external refuge; with the Dhamma as his island, the Dhamma as his refuge, seeking no other refuge?

"When he dwells contemplating the body in the body, earnestly, clearly comprehending, and mindfully, after having overcome desire and sorrow in regard to the world; when he dwells contemplating feelings in feelings, the mind in the mind, and mental objects in mental objects, earnestly, clearly comprehending, and mindfully, after having overcome desire and sorrow in regard to the world, then, truly, he is an island unto himself, a refuge unto himself, seeking no external refuge; having the Dhamma as his island, the Dhamma as his refuge, seeking no other refuge.

"Those bhikkhus of mine, Ananda, who now or after I am gone, abide as an island unto themselves, as a refuge unto themselves, seeking no other refuge; having the Dhamma as their island and refuge, seeking no other refuge: it is they who will become the highest, if they have the desire to learn."

This recorded episode from near the end of Shakyamuni's life indicates that the Buddha transferred his leadership or control over the organized sangha to all the members of the sangha itself. Accordingly, any such leader of the sangha is no more than one among equals. Further, he suggests that a sangha, to face in the same direction, must stand as individuals, not ordered around by a leader but rather united, as "islands unto themselves," in devotion to their dharma or faith.

Democracy, as practiced in the United States, is based on the equality of all people, who share the rights to life, liberty, and the pursuit of happiness. Buddhism, likewise, recognizes such inalienable rights, not in a political context, but on a fundamental level of personal liberty in which one may be free to cultivate, without fear, an enlightened condition of life.

Shakyamuni's original sangha was truly revolutionary in that in a time of strict social castes it accepted people from all walks of life. Beggars, slaves, prostitutes, and other outcasts were as welcomed as the rich and powerful. Shakyamuni instructed his novice followers to show respect to those seniors who were originally from the lower classes but had more experience in practicing the dharma. In the Buddhist sangha, people are considered noble or holy not because of their positions in society or in the sangha, but because of their consideration, compassion, humility, and devotion to the dharma and its laws.

The Dalai Lama has pointed out: "Without any apparent centralized authority Buddhism has endured for more than two thousand five hundred years." Moreover, in his view, if Buddhists lose the ability to discriminate between right and wrong, "we lose one of the basic characteristics of a human being."

This is the sort of healthy, empowered, and independent sangha that thrives within the American Tibetan Buddhist community. Although the Shambhala movement has its detractors, with some people uncomfortable with its somewhat contrived trappings of a presumed ancient Tibetan court life, most other Tibetan Buddhist sanghas are very open and aware. These practitioners make serious efforts to adhere to the Eightfold Path, as well as the Ten Precepts, all of which provides for a sound moral compass. Moreover, they recognize the advantages of an empowered sangha and are unafraid to express their personal opinions.

The Naropa University community, if anything, is on the cutting edge of such an empowered sangha. Not only do students and professors at Naropa speak their minds, but they're encouraged to do so. The administration welcomes dialogue and criticism. There is a profound respect for the founder, Trungpa Rinpoche, as well as for the Dalai Lama and younger and more current lamas like Kongtrul Rinpoche, but no one there feels compelled to bite his or her tongue or express anything less than the truth when it comes to opinions about Tibetan Buddhism or any other subject.

The case of Diamond Mountain, the Buddhist retreat center that became an object of attention after one of the expelled attendees at its three-year silence retreat died nearby of exposure, would seem to be a compelling example of a sangha that ought to stand up to question the foresight, if not the specific teachings, of its guru. Whether or not it has sufficiently done so is an open question. But there can be no argument that a Buddhist community that fails in its duty in this regard is no longer a sangha, but a cult.

Where is a modern Buddhist sangha positioned on what some sociologists refer to as the cult-sect-church spectrum? A cult can be defined as a group of religious followers that withdraws from family and society, and which directs its veneration or worship toward a particularly charismatic figure who, in turn, poses a threat to individual members of the group. Jim Jones' People's Temple, of course, is the quintessential example of a cult. A sect, on the other hand, is a group of religious followers that withdraw from family and society but with a focus on a set of religious teachings or traditions that pose no threat of harm to individual members. A Buddhist monastery, in a traditional sense, can be considered a sect. Finally, a church is a more mature, institutionalized religious body in which there are codified traditions and rules. Its members do not withdraw from society but rather seek inspiration from its teachings to live productively and happily within the world.

A lay Buddhist sangha, at least as it's expressed by most American Tibetan Buddhist groups, may be best positioned as a fourth, evolutionary step on the religious organizational spectrum. A healthy sangha requires no charismatic leader, no withdrawal from society, and no set of institutionalized rules or rituals. Rather, it is indeed a group of individuals standing as their own respective islands and leaning in the same direction—toward a dharma that is moral, awakening, pointing toward enlightenment, ultimately liberating in a personal sense, and free.

Imagine a community of faith practitioners that tolerates open dialogue, nurtures individual expression, does not impose rules or constraints on personal choice of any sort, and offers a faith consistent with scientific discovery. A sangha inspired in this way has the ability to check the excesses, if any, of its leaders, and enable the flowering of a Buddhist democracy in its truest sense.

Such a sangha is real. It's in Boulder and all across much of the American Tibetan Buddhist landscape.

10

Like Fish in Water:
The Soka Gakkai and the Mentor-Disciple Spirit

The story of the Soka Gakkai community in the United States begins on October 5, 1960, when then thirty-two-year-old Daisaku Ikeda arrives in San Francisco and stands for a photograph before Coit Tower with his traveling delegation and a small group of Japanese "war brides"—women who had married American servicemen and moved back with them to California.

At that time, the Soka Gakkai in Japan was at least two million strong, but the membership in America consisted of no more than small pockets of these so-called war brides within mostly urban areas across the country. Ikeda crisscrossed America on this first trip and met, for the most part, with these women as well as their non-Buddhist husbands. He created several Soka Gakkai chapters, appointed the women as local leaders, and gave them these following bits of practical advice: Study English, obtain driver's licenses, and become U.S. citizens. These women did just that and became the backbone of the Soka Gakkai in the United States.

By the mid-1960s, the American organization, then known as NSA, or Nichiren Shoshu of America, started to attract non-Japanese members. This coincided, of course, with the anti-Vietnam War peace movement. The introduction of faith to young Americans in those days was characterized by the organization as its "hippie to happy" movement. Spurred on by the efforts of its pioneer women members, NSA's membership grew rapidly to the extent that by the early 1970s, its newspaper, the *World Tribune*, was publishing editions three times a week.

Proselytization in those days was steady and strong. SGI meetings were held almost every night, in every major city, and members, with introductory pamphlets in hand, would fan out to street corners and malls to solicit guests. Those who were interested to join were whisked off to local temples where the Nichiren Shoshu priests—the clergy formerly associated with the Soka Gakkai—performed initiation services known as *gojukai* in which Gohonzons were bestowed and the new initiates ceremoniously tapped on the head with a scroll of the Lotus Sutra. Hundreds of thousands of Gohonzons thus were indiscriminately distributed over the thirty years leading up to around 1990. All it took was twelve dollars and a desire to say yes.

The Soka Gakkai in the United States was also distinguished in the 1970s and 1980s by the mounting of spectacular yearly conventions and cultural festivals throughout the country. At the urging of the American organization's first general director, a Japanese immigrant who adopted the name George M. Williams, each was meant to be bigger and more extravagant than the last. The planning and construction of these events required the efforts of sometimes thousands of volunteers and often took months of preparation. The 1975 convention involved the construction of a large, working volcano in the waters off Waikiki Beach, complete with exploding lava. In 1976, the organization pulled off an extraordinary electrified nighttime parade in New York City with thousands of marchers and performers. Other events, often with conspicuously patriotic themes, included the building of six-story-high human pyramids on roller skates, the assembling of a thousand-piece brass band, the construction of the world's largest chair to resemble George Washington's "rising sun" chair, and the forging of a new, working replica of the Liberty Bell—called the Freedom Bell—that toured America.

American Soka Gakkai members also made frequent pilgrimages to Japan to worship Nichiren's Dai-Gohonzon at a grand temple known as the Sho-Hondo, situated at the foot of Mount Fuji. The tours, known as *tozan*, were altogether fascinating, weird, and sublime. Williams mandated that all participants wear matching blue and white polyester suits, and groups of dozens of pilgrims would chant, out loud and in unison, during the overseas commercial flights.

The head temple grounds, known as Taiseki-ji, had been established by Nichiren's disciple, Nikko, soon after the master's death in 1282. The NSA pilgrims participated in mysterious and mystical ceremonies in which the monastics would reveal certain relics of Nichiren, including copies of his original Gosho letters or Gohonzons inscribed in his hand, which were paraded at night on the bucolic temple grounds under candlelight and twinkling stars. They would pay respect to the shrines of those three farmers persecuted long ago, as well as the grave sites of Makiguchi and Toda. The priests would whisper of fantastical stories, including their veneration of a reliquary containing one of Nichiren's actual teeth, said to be rooted, somehow, in flesh that was still alive.

These tozan events all led up to the finale—the opportunity to chant to the Dai-Gohonzon itself in the Sho-Hondo, an architectural marvel built to resemble the flight of a crane that was financed by the Soka Gakkai and opened in 1972. Despite the dramatic flair with which the monastics climbed up upon the gigantic altar and threw open the butsudan's doors, all the pomp and mystery of the head temple rituals soon subsided, and the NSA members would chant to their Dai-Gohonzon with profound sincerity. Everything else fell away—including, around 1977, the American Soka Gakkai itself.

A confluence of events brought the organization to a complete halt. American members began questioning what they perceived to be certain Japanese customs attached to the faith, as well as what they saw as an overwhelming influence of individuals in Japan over the affairs of the U.S. organization. Others, inside of the organization's top leadership, wanted Williams to be fired. Daisaku Ikeda, for his part, faced at the time a number of serious challenges in Japan, including a first attempt by the Nichiren Shoshu monastics to have him removed as Soka Gakkai leader—events that indeed led to his resignation as Soka Gakkai president in 1979. The organization in the United States was rudderless, its conventions and local meetings ceased, and thousands upon thousands of members drifted away.

Ikeda rebounded from the monastic putsch and, in a position now as Soka Gakkai International (SGI) president, again visited the United States from 1980 to 1981, met with and encouraged relatively small groups of still-active members, and set out to help rebuild the American movement. The general director, Williams, remained in control, and soon the meetings and conventions resumed at a pace that made the 1970s activities seem slow. By 1990, the organization appeared to be revitalized and brimming with new members. But Ikeda determined that not only could such growth not be sustained but that the American sangha was in danger of drifting away from Buddhism itself.

The Priesthood Issue

Starting around 1984 Ikeda cautioned, repeatedly, against the pace of the conventions and the frequency of all the NSA gatherings, concerned that they were exhausting the members and even putting them at personal risk. He counseled steady growth and the development of deepened faith among the members. Finally, in February 1990, he arrived in Los Angeles, the headquarters of the movement in the United States, and stayed put for some three weeks at the new Soka University of America campus, then in Calabasas, California. Holding daily meetings with thousands of members, Ikeda offered practical and pointed advice grounded in the teachings of Nichiren and his own mentor, Josei Toda, and produced a body of talks, speeches, and writings that would serve as a foundation for the healthy development of a renewed American organization on into the future.

In a nutshell, he asked everyone to slow down. Faith, he noted, equals daily life: as valuable as religious activities might be, every aspect of each person's daily life, as well, is equally important. He clarified that the point of Nichiren's teachings was to become happy; that Buddhism is about having compassion and consideration for all people; that it emphasizes living a balanced life in accordance with the Middle Way; and that practitioners are free to determine the direction of their lives, based on faith, on what is in their respective hearts, and on how they choose as individuals to respond to their mentor. Within the year, Williams stepped down as general director.

The newly coined SGI-USA became further free to develop into the healthy organization it ultimately became following the excommunication of the millions of Soka Gakkai members by Nichiren Shoshu in 1991.

Gone was the drumbeat by the monastics for more members and more money.

Cancelled were the pilgrimages to Japan.

Away went Nichiren's tooth, along with other mysterious and illogical rituals, including the fetish of the Dai-Gohonzon.

Banished were many Japanese customs associated with the organization, including the embarrassing habit by Americans to break into "banzai" types of cheers.

Demolished even, in a fit of pique by Nichiren Shoshu's high priest, was the architecturally significant Sho-Hondo building.

In place was the opportunity to build, finally, an American SGI sangha.

The many million member strong Soka Gakkai, finding itself with no clergy, essentially became the first international, laity-led, protestant Buddhist movement in the 2,600 year old history of the faith.[7] Following Nichiren's prescription that "for your regular recitation, I recommend that you practice reading the prose sections of the 'Expedient Means' and 'Life Span' chapters" of the Lotus Sutra, the layperson leaders of the SGI, under Ikeda's watch, reduced the group's daily recommended liturgy from a series of prayers that took thirty minutes to perform to a more essential liturgy for busy people that could be recited in five minutes. The gigantic and exhaustive yearly conventions were done away with. Meetings were no longer held every night but discussion meetings were now scheduled once a month. Study meetings, formerly ignored, were now emphasized, also on a monthly schedule. Efforts in propagating the faith became more natural and much less neurotic, and new members were required to express a determined desire to join and begin practicing before receiving a Gohonzon. Although, as with all Buddhist sanghas, estimates are difficult to make, today there are perhaps 100,000 active SGI-USA members served through some one hundred cultural centers and other buildings and facilities throughout the country.

The Inverted Pyramid

The key public arena for SGI-USA members to come together is what's known as the discussion meeting. These are local meetings, for anywhere from ten to thirty people, held once a month in members' homes. Meetings begin with the recitation of the liturgy, followed by a few minutes of chanting *Nam-myoho-renge-kyo*. The meetings themselves usually include an explanation of

---

7. A few dozen Japanese priests who had sided with the Soka Gakkai in its dispute with Nichiren Shoshu departed the monastic order and now support the layperson group.

the practice, one or two experiences in faith by SGI-USA members, a study portion in which the writings of Nichiren or Daisaku Ikeda are shared, a brief artistic presentation—perhaps a musical performance, a song or the recitation of a poem—offered by one of the members, and then a question and answer session with a senior leader in the group. The discussion meetings are the beating heart of the Soka Gakkai. They're typically described as oases: gatherings of often very genuine common people seeking to encourage each other in faith.

The SGI-USA appears to be structured in a very hierarchical manner but this is mostly designed for purposes of communication. Positions of leadership are basically offered to anyone who has an interest in caring for others. Typically, the smallest unit is at the "group" level, which might include ten people. The "district" leaders care for the district, and from there the leadership positions start to fulfill more of an administrative function. There are chapter leaders, area leaders, region leaders, and territory leaders, for men, women, young men, and young women, all the way up to the general director position. These more senior leaders are in positions to offer guidance in faith to junior members, to plan larger activities, and to relay information throughout the organization.

The entire Soka Gakkai is configured as an inverted pyramid. The mass of members is at the top, and the most senior of leaders—those with the most responsibility for others—are at the bottom, at the point of the pyramid. Buddhist leaders, as emphasized by Daisaku Ikeda, are meant to serve others. Ikeda's constant and voluminous guidance on the subject of leadership provides not only a clear path for the Soka Gakkai sangha, but a collection of it would likely offer graduate-level management coursework applicable to any endeavor. Not surprisingly, his writings and remarks on the subject are generally consistent with the anti-authoritarian positions of his mentors, Makiguchi and Toda. The following samples reflect his thoughts in this regard:

- *Leaders need to value those who offer opinions.* According to Ikeda, growth and development requires change and innovation. Innovation can't take place if fresh ideas are ignored or suppressed. He emphasizes that successful leaders are those who are open-minded enough to accept constructive opinions.

- *Leaders must not become so preoccupied with the organization's workings or its hierarchy that they begin to view members as a faceless mass.* Ikeda has repeatedly stated his belief that everyone is fundamentally equal, and it is critical to respect the feelings of each individual. Moreover, members don't exist for the sake of their Buddhist leaders; rather, the organization exists for the members.

- *It is by overcoming difficulties that one becomes a Buddha.* To Ikeda, and to Buddhists in general, difficulties are an honor. Moreover, one's personal struggle against difficulties and obstacles is itself the core of leadership training.

- *Should any self-serving or arrogant leaders emerge, it is vital that you speak out and correct them.* Ikeda has pointed out that, from the time of Makiguchi, the Soka Gakkai has always been driven from the bottom up and that members should be encouraged to say what's on their minds. Ikeda has further stressed that leaders shouldn't order members about; that they ought to be strict with themselves but gentle toward their fellow members; wage an earnest personal struggle, while taking the pressure off of others; and set examples of hard work, while relieving others of their fatigue.

The emphasis on leadership in the SGI-USA cuts two ways. On the one hand, it's an ingenious structure because it immediately places any willing novice practitioner in the position of having to care for fellow members of the sangha. Thus, there's no lip service in the organization about caring for others *after* achieving some elevated state of life. Instead, consistent with the Mahayana ideal of bodhisattva practice, an SGI member starts to care for others right away. In the SGI, such care comes *before* any pretense to enlightenment. More to the point, caring for others is viewed as the very cause for spiritual improvement.

On the other hand, the appointment of so many, many "senior leaders" can result in a rather bloated sort of Buddhist leadership bureaucracy. Of course, from a Buddhist viewpoint, no one person is inherently more valuable than any other practitioner, and one's position couldn't be any less important from the perspective of Buddha nature and enlightenment. But there can be peculiar effects on your ego when you walk to a podium and invariably several hundred people clap. In such a receptive environment, you can really start to believe that you know what Buddhism is about—even if you don't.

At times, consistent with human nature, cliques of SGI-USA leaders would exhibit an imperious approach, despite Ikeda's forceful messages to the contrary. Gay and lesbian members, for example, had to put up a considerable fight some years ago to be open and fully welcomed within the organization—a struggle well worth the effort, as they're embraced by the SGI-USA today more than perhaps any other American religious organization, whether Buddhist or not. Similarly, African American members over the years expressed a sense of marginalization from higher-level leadership positions. Also, with so many leaders asserting their responsibilities to take charge, the SGI-USA membership tends to be more passive and less activist or independent than the American Tibetan Buddhist sanghas in the context of checking and balancing leadership excesses. With respect to organizational matters, differences of opinion, in general, are less tolerated in the SGI-USA. A focus on the appearance of ironclad unity is at times especially pronounced.

Such an ethos, however, will likely evolve toward greater openness and freedom of expression. Quite apart from Ikeda wanting it to be so, the single biggest promise of such evolution is that the people drawn to attend SGI-USA meetings are remarkably diverse. The late Buddhist scholar David Chappell commented on this phenomenon in his study, *Racial Diversity in the Soka Gakkai:* "This universal affirmation of the value of every human being is found in Buddhism, Christianity, and Islam, but the way Soka Gakkai applied this principle to all strata of society without demanding a change in their lifestyle, was exceptional and represents a distinctive feature."

Racial Diversity

The SGI-USA, top to bottom, is by far the most ethnically and economically diverse Buddhist group in the United States. Its current top three leaders are, respectively, a Pakistani-American man, an African American woman and a Japanese-American man. The SGI-USA reflects what Shakyamuni many centuries ago described as the ideal Buddhist sangha: one that is open to the rich and powerful, as well as to the downtrodden, the oppressed, and even the criminal classes. An SGI-USA meeting is a literal human rainbow and includes people representing every spectrum of our common experience. Gay or straight, black or white, Asian or Hispanic, young or old, disabled or not—they're all there. One religion writer estimated in *Tricycle* that African Americans, alone, comprise twenty percent of the group's membership. A typical Sunday at an SGI-USA cultural center might include a large chanting session in one room, a Spanish-language meeting in another, a children's group in yet another area, and band practices in the building's basement. It is a cacophony that would be welcomed by any other Buddhist sangha.

What sets apart the SGI-USA from other Buddhist groups in the realm of diversity? For one thing, it's not expensive to practice its teachings. Apart from the minimal application fee to receive the Gohonzon, most meetings for SGI-USA members and their friends are utterly free of charge. The only fees that would be assessed apply to room and board at optional weekend retreats held at a Florida center maintained by the organization, or tuition fees associated with admission at the small and now highly competitive Soka University of America, near Los Angeles. Although approximately eighty percent of the SGI-USA operating budget derives from member contributions, there is no tithing or requirement that any member has to donate. In other words, the class and economic barriers affecting prospective Zen and Tibetan Buddhists are nonexistent in the Soka Gakkai.

© David Bartolomi.

SGI-USA members typically meet in practitioners' homes. An altar housing the Gohonzon is on the left, in the background.

More notably, the actual Buddhist practice of the SGI-USA, as compared to Zen and Tibetan Buddhism, is far more accessible to people with both feet planted firmly in the confusion of daily life. If anything, Nichiren, unlike other historically great and influential monks, held that enlightenment can *only* be found in the midst of worldly affairs.

According to Nichiren's Buddhism, and as taught to the Soka Gakkai by Daisaku Ikeda and his earlier mentors, the world of enlightenment is accessed by chanting *Nam-myoho-renge-kyo* to the Gohonzon and engaging in bodhisattva practice. There is no complicated cosmology to learn, no secret tantric teaching, no mystical power available only to monastics, and no gritty practice of meditation to master before tasting the sweet nectar of enlightenment. As long as one's prayer is sincere, it happens as soon as a practitioner sits down to chant. Anyone with a blank wall on which to position the Gohonzon can do this. It is this efficacy of practice, more than anything, that attracts a naturally diverse sangha.

Earlier critics of the Soka Gakkai relentlessly disparaged the organization as barely even Buddhist. Some look down their noses, for example, at the prosaic notion of a down-on-her-luck woman chanting for more money, as if that's no road to enlightenment. But "earthly desires are enlightenment" means just that. If there's something someone needs, and one needs it badly enough, then that person will sit before her mandala and chant until she finds the courage, energy, and wisdom to pull it out of the universe. If zazen for Zen Buddhists is a desperate fight to know oneself, chanting daimoku for Soka Gakkai members is no less of a struggle leading ultimately to the same result: enlightenment—or, if you will, fearlessness. As Ikeda often says, Buddhism is win or lose. If our poor woman gets that money to feed her children, let's say, she'll next seek to achieve something even larger in her life. The more she chants, and the greater her resulting benefits, the more intense her faith becomes. The prayer of such an SGI-USA member, accordingly, deepens over time. The person who started by chanting for something as trivial as a better parking spot is transformed into someone who prays for others' happiness, chants simply for the love of chanting, masters and learns to direct his or her desires toward more valuable ends, and is at peace with his or her indestructible and eternally true self.

Celebrity SGI members

Such members, of course, don't walk around looking like Buddhas. Rather, some of the more conspicuous ones resemble Tina Turner, Herbie Hancock, and the actor Orlando Bloom. Turner, as portrayed famously in her biopic *What's Love Got To Do With It*, started to practice Buddhism by praying to escape the beatings administered to her by her husband Ike. Hancock, the jazz virtuoso, is a long-time Soka Gakkai member and mid-level organization leader. As part of an interview published on the Beliefnet website, Hancock observed:

> *This practice of Buddhism has given me several realizations. One of the most important ones is to realize finally that this thing that I've been kind of placing up on a pedestal, sort of as my object of worship—music and being a musician—I wasn't looking at it the true way. I realized that being a musician is not what I am, it's what I do. I'm also a father, I'm a son, I'm a neighbor, I'm a citizen, I'm an African American. I'm a bunch of things. But, at the center of all of that is I'm a human being. Now I view music from the standpoint of being a human being rather than being a musician. So, that's a much deeper overview.*

True to the legacy left by Makiguchi and Toda, the Soka Gakkai has established in the United States a number of educational institutes and peace initiatives. These include Soka University of America, which is, like Naropa University, a Buddhist-inspired nonsectarian school of higher education. Following a drawn-out land-use fight in the 1990s over its proposed expansion on an already developed scenic plot in the Santa Monica Mountains—a fight one State official once compared to the "park equivalent of thermonuclear war"—the accredited four-year college and graduate school finally opened its doors in Aliso Viejo, California, in 2001, to its first undergraduate students. Founded by Daisaku Ikeda, its liberal arts educational philosophy is based on the principles of peace, human rights, and the sanctity of life. The state of the art campus offers an enviable nine-to-one student-faculty ratio, and all students, now hailing from more than forty different countries, are required to spend their junior year studying overseas.

The Soka Gakkai International is an active nongovernmental organization with formal consultative relations with the United Nations. The Ikeda Center for Peace, Learning, and Dialogue, in Cambridge, Massachusetts, brings together multidisciplinary scholars in the search for dialogue and the discovery of "solutions that will assist in the peaceful evolution of humanity." The SGI-USA's Florida Nature and Culture Center provides faith retreats for SGI members throughout the Americas.

What matters most, though, is the mentor-student, or, in the parlance of the Soka Gakkai, the mentor-disciple spirit. Regardless of what grand buildings are left behind, if this fundamental point is missed, Buddhism in serious trouble. This relationship, whether in Zen, Vajrayana or the Soka Gakkai, is the epitome of Buddhism.

Forever Sensei

Within the SGI-USA community there's no talk of "emptiness" or "awakening" in a Zen or Tibetan Buddhist sense. Instead one hears a lot of the following phrases: "life force," "life condition," "happiness," "courage," "benefit," "human revolution," and "cause and effect." Such a lexicon derives from the speeches and talks of Daisaku Ikeda, often referred to by SGI-USA members simply as "Sensei."

The mentoring model offered to SGI-USA members is drawn from the relationship between Ikeda and his mentor, Josei Toda, and the relationship between Toda and Tsunesaburo Makiguchi. Recalling his mentoring relationship with Toda, Ikeda has said:

> *I took his each and every word very, very seriously. If the disciples do not carry out their mentor's words, they render them empty and meaningless, and they are only masquerading as disciples. . . . Thus, it all comes down to whether we have the spirit to deeply make the vision and intent of our mentor our own—no matter how casually those words may have been mentioned in passing—and to keep them shining brightly in our hearts like diamonds and polishing them constantly as we endeavor to make them a reality. This is the solemn path of mentor and disciple.*

If anything is holding back Buddhism from developing more soundly or spreading more rapidly in America it's the resistance so many people have to the mentor-disciple concept. In light of history, though—including Western history, it's the shared struggle of the mentor and the disciples that allows great philosophies and teachings to endure. For example, one need not look any further than Socrates, Plato, and Aristotle. From the perspective of those within such a relationship, there is no greater fortune than being able to encounter an individual selflessly dedicated to the truth and filled with wisdom and compassion. Obviously, in this endeavor, it's vital to wisely choose whom to follow.

In the world of the Soka Gakkai, with Ikeda as the practical mentor and Nichiren and the Gohonzon as the eternal one, true character is forged through meeting the real-life challenges of hardship and suffering. When coupled with chanting, this process, known as human revolution, leads to enlightenment much as the hammering of a sword removes its impurities. This is no abstract theory. Rather, by seeking to learn and put into practice what the mentor teaches, a person can realize humility, self-improvement, achievement, and victory in the truest sense. Importantly, it's not a relationship based at all on authority or power but rather one grounded in inspiration. In Josei Toda's words, "The relationship between a mentor and disciple is as profound and inseparable as fish and water. The mentor cherishes and guides the disciple, and the disciple respects and admires the mentor. No human sentiment is more beautiful."

The Buddha's vow to make all people equal to him in the context of enlightenment cannot be fulfilled by the Buddha alone. It also depends on how much the disciples who have heard the dharma actually exert themselves in their Buddhist practice with a sense of appreciation and resolve to live up to their teacher's aspirations for them. This is the key. The way of mentor and disciple is not complete unless the flame of gratitude burns in the disciples' hearts. Interestingly, this requires on the part of a disciple courage and independence— qualities most cherished by Westerners—rather than meekness and dependency. It also requires the arrest and control of one's ego. And although it all comes down to the intensity of the practitioner's resolve, it turns out that such utterly committed determination and actions to seek out the teacher are the sources of limitless strength. Ultimately, the student or disciple, in whichever Buddhist tradition, learns to take the mentor's spirit and goals as one's own, engraves them in his or her heart, and thinks about what must be done.

As any Buddhist practitioner will agree, this isn't easy to do. And the SGI-USA, like its Zen and Vajrayana counterparts in America, doesn't push it. It will encourage its members to study and learn more about Daisaku Ikeda, but with the recognition that it's up to the individual, whenever he or she is ready, to decide that pursuing the oneness of mentor and disciple should be a primary quest of life.

This is the reality of the SGI-USA. Although the organization and its members have been criticized, mostly in years past, either for superficiality, an aversion to monastics, or even for cultlike behaviors, the truth is that what's really happening at its cultural centers, its discussion meetings, and before every Gohonzon to which its individual members pray is a magnificent drama between mentor and disciple—one that's directed toward happiness, victory, and enlightenment.

Conclusion:
In the Next Present Moment: The Future of Buddhism in America

It took Buddhism about a thousand years to migrate from India to China, Vietnam, Tibet, and other Asian lands, and another five hundred years or so thereafter to spread meaningfully into Korea and Japan. As it deepened its roots in each of these new cultures, the teachings were transformed and adapted to accommodate the changing times and peoples. Throughout its 2,600 years, Buddhism has proven to be a remarkably adaptable faith. As it's only been about fifty years since the dharma significantly penetrated into the United States, there's presumably a long, long way to go before the story of an evolving, American-infused Buddhism can truly be told.

Obviously, the world today is a lot smaller than it was in Shakyamuni's day, and our technological advances, relative to the distant past, will surely help speed the development of the American Buddhist phenomenon. And although Buddhism carries with it a distinctly Asian, inductive approach to interpreting life, death, and the meaning of it all, it also possesses unique attributes that promise a future prospering of the faith in the deductive West. Among these qualities are the relative ease of practice, the independence afforded to practitioners who seek to apply the dharma to their daily lives, and the consistency of the philosophy with respect to scientific inquiry. Not to mention, of course, that for many Buddhist practice unquestionably "works."

Each of the Zen, Tibetan, and Soka Gakkai schools had a predictably bumpy start in America. Both Zen and Tibetan Buddhism wrestled early on with problems relating to some serious sexual indiscretions and other corruptive influences. American Zen practitioners, as well, have had to rewrite Zen's place in an ethical universe, particularly on the heels of its immediately preceding Japanese moral indiscretions. The Soka Gakkai, for its part, struggled over its first thirty years to find an appropriate and healthy balance between monastic, missionary zeal and a layperson's daily life. In addition, much more than was required of Zen or Tibetan Buddhism, the Soka Gakkai has fought to define itself, with mixed results, as a serious and legitimate Buddhist movement in the face of onslaughts from its former clergy and a generally hostile popular and academic press.

A study released a few years ago by the Pew Forum on Religion and Public Life found that only about half of Americans who are raised as Buddhists retain their faith into adulthood. This low rate presumably applies more to children of Asian-Americans raised in their indigenous faith than to those of American converts who comprise the majority of Buddhists in the United States today, but there's clearly a challenge observed concerning the evolution of Buddhism over the span of subsequent generations. For one thing, there may very well be a reluctance on the part of first-generation, baby-boomer Buddhist converts to pass along their practices to their children, but the bigger challenge seems to be that American Buddhism, collectively, hasn't yet settled on an American identity or even, in the case of Zen, whether that identity should be that of a religion.

Some Buddhist scholars and highly respected translators, such as Alexander Berzin and Ken McLeod, have observed that a misunderstanding of Buddhism in the West derives in part from mistranslations into English of key Buddhist texts and concepts. McLeod, in particular, has devoted much of his career to exploring how to best communicate Buddhist tenets to contemporary Americans. Trained in Tibetan Buddhism, McLeod in the late 1980s moved away from the traditional master-student approach and, while incorporating perspectives from Zen and Theravada Buddhism, along with psychology, started what he calls Unfettered Mind. His primary inquiry in this regard is to work with individual practitioners to reach the fundamental essence of

Buddhist teachings by distinguishing and separating out what's Buddhism and what's merely cultural baggage.

This is no easy task. The SGI-USA, for example, has debated this question throughout its entire existence. Does loyalty to an SGI-USA senior leader, for example, derive from the mentor-disciple relationship, or is it a carryover from a Japanese *bushido* ethic? Can an American SGI member adhere to Nichiren's prescription to the sangha concerning *itai doshin*, or "many in body, one in mind," yet, if in disagreement with some organizational policy, still maintain his or her unfettered rights to freedom of opinion and speech? Likewise, could a Tibetan Buddhist devote himself to the tenets of his faith yet, without recrimination, be overtly critical of a political position taken by the Dalai Lama? Can dokusan, in Zen, still be effective without having to prostrate oneself three times before the master? All of these questions are indicative of the struggle by Americans to find, in context with the culture from which they spring, an authentic Buddhist practice with the depth and resonance traditionally associated with monastic Buddhism.

A Buddhist concept known in Japanese as *zuiho bini* suggests that the teachings are free to adapt to local customs. In other words, in matters the Buddha did not expressly either permit or forbid, one may act in accordance with a resident culture as long as the fundamental principles of Buddhism are not violated. This precept, of course, has been employed throughout history as Buddhism made its way to various nations or regions that differed in matters of culture, manners, climate, and other natural and human aspects. Buddhism, an extraordinarily flexible faith when it comes to social mores, incorporated Bon traditions as it entered Tibet, Taoist and Confucian principles in China, and something of a samurai or even nationalistic outlook in Japan. The now ubiquitous existence of iconic statues of the Buddha itself came from cross-pollinating Buddhist teachings with the polytheistic notions of ancient Greek merchants. In America, most conspicuously, Zen, for the first time in its 1,500-year history, is in the midst of developing a real-world ethical perspective.

To thrive in the United States, Zen, as well as Tibetan Buddhism to some extent, has to figure out how to expand its appeal beyond a mostly white, educated and relatively well-to-do constituency. Cost and the considerable time commitment necessary to succeed in these practices remain significant obstacles to attracting the sort of very diverse sangha that Shakyamuni, long ago, envisioned and described. Perhaps Tibetan Buddhism, through its easily accessed Shambhala centers, has a leg up in this respect: some of their programs are free of charge, although others, particularly those including food and lodging, can be relatively pricey.

The Soka Gakkai, on the other hand, presents a much more accessible and easy approach to practicing Buddhism. There are virtually no costs required, and its dharma, while profound, is centered on simply chanting the phrase *Nam-myoho-renge-kyo* to a Gohonzon. Its thoroughly diverse community of believers is evidence enough that it's on the right track in this regard. Still, the SGI-USA, despite Daisaku Ikeda's admonitions to the contrary, at times continues to face the challenges of maintaining the proper balance between strong, centralized management and the toleration of constructive, internal criticism. Nevertheless, the organization will certainly continue to develop in the direction of greater openness as a result of its naturally increasing diversity and as a function of more members connecting directly to the guidance offered by their mentor. It would sure be a heck of a strong Buddhist movement, for example, if one could somehow take the ethos of personal liberty exhibited by the Tibetan Buddhist sangha and combine that with the accessible teachings and wise mentoring offered by the Soka Gakkai.

Ultimately, though, the success of any Buddhist school in America has little to do with institutional or social reforms. In fact, it has little to do with the umbrella organizations at all. Rather, in view of Thich Nhat Hanh's prescient and poetic observation that the next Buddha is itself the sangha, the success of Buddhism in the United States is predicated on each individual practitioner. If the Americans who come to Buddhism are sincere in their faith, and if each of them keeps a focus on studying, practicing, and believing in the dharma, then the leadership of each movement—whether clerical, monastic, or layperson—is of only secondary concern. The key, as foreseen by Shakyamuni long ago, is for people to be islands of dharma unto themselves. Such islands, if you will, each bear different fragrances, flowers, vegetation, and beachheads, but together— united in dharma, devoted to their mentor—they form archipelagoes of consideration, fearlessness, happiness, and peace.

As much as Buddhism still needs to adapt to America, America needs this dharma. Plagued as we are with issues of personal and collective violence, as well as a culture of blame, Americans will find that Buddhism offers a clear way forward. This path still needs to be pruned here and there, but it is well trodden and direct. Buddhism, moreover, isn't an "ism" in a theoretically political or social sense. Nothing externally has to change.

Only "I" do.

The Buddhist way to personal enlightenment and global peace is all about what Daisaku Ikeda, for one, refers to as human revolution: that a great revolution within even one person will help achieve a change in the destiny of all humankind.

Afterword

Back in 1995, after some twelve years of Buddhist practice, I was reeling and didn't have the slightest clue anymore about what was supposed to make me happy. To be specific, I lost pretty much everything that my happiness was *attached* to: the blonde girlfriend whom I had married and who was soon to become my ex-wife, our house with a two-car garage on a mountaintop in California, a meaningful job, my interest in faith, and even my loyal, long-haired dachshund. For lack of anything better to do, and in a confused state of mind spinning with questions about what went wrong, I half-heartedly accepted an invitation to come to Japan, the home of Zen and Soka Gakkai Buddhism.

I recall having had a hurtful fight with my wife on the way to the airport, after which she was left in tears. The overseas flight was turbulent, and I'm not an especially relaxed flyer. At one point over the Pacific Ocean the pilot felt compelled to inform us all that an upcoming patch of air might be particularly rough and that, as if it would help, we needed to hold on. Upon arrival in Tokyo I learned that my bags had been sent to Osaka. I really didn't want to be in Japan.

Along with some Soka Gakkai colleagues, I was scheduled to participate the next morning in a large monthly meeting to be attended by SGI President Daisaku Ikeda in Makiguchi Memorial Hall, near Soka University, in the city of Hachioji. I was also told that Mr. Ikeda, whom I then casually referred to as "my mentor," would like to meet with me prior to the gathering, a bit of information that I considered very likely to be untrue.

For years I had poured out my heart to him in letters and typically had not received any response whatsoever. And with things not going as well as planned in my life, I felt abandoned at what I thought was my time of crisis by my so-called mentor. In retrospect, I realize that mentors have a way of knowing what their students or disciples in fact need.

I did meet Mr. Ikeda that morning, and I went on to either see or correspond with him continuously over the next ten weeks during my stay in Japan. I still can't quite explain why this occurred, as I was not, and still am not, anywhere close to some sort of fabulous disciple. I did, however, observe firsthand who Daisaku Ikeda is. For one thing, I saw with my own eyes that this man bears no resemblance whatsoever to the generally superficial reports published about him and recirculated mostly in the popular or tabloid press over the past fifty years. More importantly, with no shred of any lingering doubt, I came to know him as a mentor in the truest sense of the word.

Finding this sort of person and engraving his spirit and words in your life—essentially striving to make a mentor's heart your own—is the essence of Buddhism. I was thickheaded and arrogant enough to have to have been in my mentor's presence for me to see this for myself, but there are many millions of individuals, more humble than me, who need to read or hear as little as a sentence from someone to know that they've found a person worthy to be their teacher. It's difficult for those outside such a relationship to understand, but, for me, finding my mentor is in a sense even more fulfilling than later finding the person I truly loved. As it was, discovering my true love came as a direct result of my relationship with my mentor, but that's, as they say, a whole 'nother story.

I'm sure I'm not the only so-called Buddhist disciple who feels this way. Among the many Tibetan Buddhists I met are numerous accomplished and well-spoken individuals who revel in the joy of having found their teacher, whether it be the Dalai Lama, Dzigar Kongtrul Rinpoche or someone else. In particular, I've noted with a distant sense of recognition the poignant words of appreciation that Pema Chodron always has for her mentor, Chogyam Trungpa Rinpoche, despite the fact that he died many years ago and had been the subject of considerable criticism and even ridicule while he was alive. John Daido Loori throughout his life was devoted to his mentor, Taizan Maezumi Roshi, even though the latter struggled with alcohol dependency and extramarital affairs. And Daido's own dharma heirs at the Mountains and Rivers Order today are furthering the precise Buddhist path that Daido himself first cut.

I hesitate, as I write, to even share details about Daisaku Ikeda, because my experiences in this regard are personal, and I don't at all want anyone to think that I consider myself to be special in any way. As with most profound lessons in life, I learned the hard way that I'm decidedly not.

Still, I would want to shout out loud about who Daisaku Ikeda really is—how he thanks people to such an extent that it almost overwhelms them. When the late Rosa Parks, the great "Mother of the Civil Rights Movement," visited Mr. Ikeda in Japan in 1994, the bouquets of flowers he offered her filled the entrance to her room. Thousands of Japanese students at Soka Women's Junior College, a school Mr. Ikeda founded, serenaded her in broken English upon her arrival by spontaneously lining a road into the campus and singing *We Shall Overcome.* I would want people to know that Daisaku Ikeda, during my stay in Japan, took the time out of his busy schedule to learn in great detail about my ancestors who perished in the Holocaust, as well as my other relatives who suffered in a twentieth-century conflagration of fascism, Communism, and other misplaced nationalistic faiths. I would tell people that he speaks, always from the perspective of Buddhism as taught to him by his mentor, Josei Toda, on topics as diverse as happiness, astronomy, history, love, and even the New York Yankees. But it's hard to get that message through. The Buddhist notion of mentoring appears to some in the West to be an even frightening concept. More specifically, a lot of people looking in from the outside are inclined to malign most religious leaders and project onto them their fears of mass movements, politics, or even cults.

Somehow, throughout all my prior years of practice, I had completely missed the point of Buddhism. It's not simply about benefit, or poetry, or leadership; it's not about extinguishing desire, or becoming empty, or learning to be fully awake; and it's not solely about courage or peace or morality. Above all, Buddhism, in my view, and from a practical perspective, really isn't even about enlightenment—a concept that's so poorly defined and so difficult to sustain as to be abstract.

I finally made Daisaku Ikeda my mentor in the truest sense when I realized, from his example, that what Buddhism is about is caring for others under any circumstance: real and profound care, appreciation and respect for each individual you meet as if you were meeting the Buddha himself.

In the end, the mentor-student relationship in Buddhism is utterly personal. There's a concept attributed to the ancient Buddhist master Nagarjuna called, in Japanese, *hendoku iyaku*. Literally meaning "change poison, make medicine," it stands for the fact that suffering can be transformed into benefit and enlightenment by virtue of the power of the Law. This isn't something that just happens because you chant or meditate. Instead, it suggests more of a brutal, gradual, and honest process of self-reflection in which you, based on Buddhist practice, and with inspiration and direction from your mentor, take responsibility for all that affects your life. It has everything to do with identifying, capturing, and ultimately controlling your own ego. It has nothing to do with what anybody else might think.

I'm no longer a leader in the SGI-USA, but I am a Buddhist. I chant *Nam-myoho-renge-kyo* to my Gohonzon, I am a disciple of Daisaku Ikeda, and I try to the best of my ability to live a good and creative life consistent with the three-thousand-year-old notion of bodhisattva practice.

Life and all of its phenomena, as Shakyamuni himself first taught, is impermanent and constantly changing. But thanks to the practice of Buddhism, my life, with all its ups and downs, in the long run just keeps getting better—more appreciative, more secure, and more confident. I now live with my new wife, our three children, and, in my heart, my mentor on our mundane and exquisitely ordinary own little island of dharma. There's nothing that particularly distinguishes the five of us from anyone else, and for the most part we're just left alone by the world. Yet for some reason, when I approach my Buddhist altar each morning, I feel happier than the day that came before.

Resources

Websites

For general information about Soto Zen Buddhism:
http://szba.org

For general information about Rinzai Zen Buddhism:
http://www.rinzaizen.org/

For the Zen Mountain Monastery and the Mountains and Rivers Order:
http://mro.org/

For general information about Tibetan Buddhism:
http://www.tibethouse.us/

For information about Shambhala meditation:
http://www.shambhala.org/

For information about Naropa University:
http://www.naropa.edu/

For information about the Soka Gakkai International-USA:
http://sgi-usa.org/

For further information about the SGI and its history and philosophy:
http://www.sgi.org/

For information about Soka University of America:
http://soka.edu/

Recommended Reading

Chodron, Pema, *Living Beautifully: with Uncertainty and Change*, Shambhala, 2012.

H.H. the Dalai Lama, Howard C. Cutler, *The Art of Happiness, 10th Anniversary Edition: A Handbook for Living*, Riverhead, 2009.

H.H. the Dalai Lama, Nicholas Vreeland, *An Open Heart: Practicing Compassion in Everyday Life*, Back Bay Books, 2002.

Dilgo Khyentse, Konchog Tenzin, trans., *The Wish-Fulfilling Jewel*, Shambhala, 1988.

The Gosho Translation Committee, ed., *The Writings of Nichiren Daishonin*, Soka Gakkai, 1999.

Habito, Ruben L.F., *Experiencing Buddhism: Ways of Wisdom and Compassion*, Orbis Books, 2005.

Hammond, Philip, David Machacek, *Soka Gakkai in America: Accommodation and Conversion*, Oxford University Press, 1999.

Hochswender, Woody, Greg Martin, Ted Morino, *The Buddha in Your Mirror: Practical Buddhism and the Search for Self*, Middleway Press, 2001.

Hurst, Jane D., *Nichiren Shoshu Buddhism and the Soka Gakkai in America: The Ethos of a New Religious Movement*, Garland Publishing, 1992.

Ikeda, Daisaku, *The Human Revolution*, World Tribune Press, 2004.

Ikeda, Daisaku, *Unlocking the Mysteries of Birth and Death: . . . And Everything In Between*, Middleway Press, 2004.

Ikeda, Daisaku, Katsuji Saito, Takanori Endo, Haruo Suda, *The Wisdom of the Lotus Sutra: A Discussion*, vols. 1-6, World Tribune Press, 2000.

Ives, Christopher, *Zen Awakening and Society,* University of Hawaii Press, 1992.

Kongtrul, Dzigar, *It's Up to You*, Shambhala, 2005.

Kongtrul, Jamgon, Ken McLeod, trans., *The Great Path of Awakening*, Shambhala, 1987.

Loori, John Daido, *The Eight Gates of Zen*, Shambhala, 2002.

McLeod, Ken, *Wake Up To Your Life: Discovering the Buddhist Path of Attention*, HarperOne, 2002.

Padma Sambhava, Robert Thurman, trans., *The Tibetan Book of the Dead: The Great Book of Natural Liberation Through Understanding in the Between*, Bantam Books, 1993.

Page, Dr. Tony, Kosho Yamamoto, trans., *The Mahayana Mahaparinirvana Sutra*, F. Lepine Publishing, 2008.

Prebish, Charles S., Kenneth K. Tanaka, eds., *The Faces of Buddhism in America*, University of California Press, 1998.

Seager, Richard Hughes, *Buddhism in America, Revised and Expanded* (Columbia Contemporary American Religious Series), Columbia University Press, 2012.

Seager, Richard Hughes, *Encountering the Dharma: Daisaku Ikeda, Soka Gakkai, and the Globalization of Buddhist Humanism*, University of California Press, 2006.

Sharma, Nirmala, *Kumarajiva: The Transcreator of Buddhist Chinese Diction*, Niyogi Books, 2011.

Sister Vajira, Francis Story, *Last Days of the Buddha: The Maha Parinibbana Sutta,* rev. ed., Buddhist Publication Society, 2007.

Suzuki, D.T., *An Introduction to Zen Buddhism*, Grove Press, 1964.

Thich Nhat Hanh, *The Heart of the Buddha's Teaching*, Broadway Books, 1998.

Thich Nhat Hanh, Arnold Kotler, *Peace Is Every Step: The Path of Mindfulness in Everyday Life*, Bantam Books, 1992.

Tricycle, *The Buddhist Review* (a monthly magazine in the United States devoted to Buddhist news and the Buddhist community).

Trungpa, Chogyam, *Shambhala: The Sacred Path of the Warrior*, Shambhala, 2007.

Victoria, Brian Daizen, *Zen At War*, 2nd ed., Rowman & Littlefield Publishers, 2006.

Wang-Ch'ug Dorje, Alexander Berzin, trans., *The Mahamudra*, The Library of Tibetan Works & Archives, 1978.

Warner, Brad, *Hard Core Zen: Punk Rock, Monster Movies and the Truth About Reality*, Wisdom Publications, 2003.

Watson, Burton, trans., *The Lotus Sutra*, Columbia University Press, 1993.

Yampolsky, Philip, ed., Burton Watson, et al., trans., *Selected Writings of Nichiren*, Columbia University Press, 1990.

Glossary

BARDO THODOL: Otherwise known as the Tibetan Book of the Dead, it describes the experiences one is said to encounter after death.

BODHICITTA: The practice of compassion for others in Tibetan Buddhism.

BODHISATTVA: A person of great compassion who is close to attaining enlightenment.

BODHI TREE: The large fig tree in India under which Shakyamuni sat and attained enlightenment.

BUTSUDAN: A protective box on an altar into which a mandala or Gohonzon is placed.

CRAZY WISDOM: A method of tantric teaching, attributed, among others, to Chogyam Trungpa Rinpoche, in which the mentor behaves in unconventional, outrageous, or unexpected fashion.

DAIMOKU: A word used at times to refer to *Nam-myoho-renge-kyo*.

DEPENDENT ORIGINATION: A concept expressing the notion that everything in the universe is interconnected and not existing in isolation.

DHARMA: Generally referring to the Law of the universe and specifically to the teachings of Buddhism.

DHARMA TRANSMISSION: In Zen, a custom in which an experienced practitioner is established as an heir to an unbroken lineage of teachers and disciples said to be traced back to Shakyamuni.

DIAMOND MOUNTAIN UNIVERSITY: A Tibetan Buddhism-related retreat in Arizona.

DIAMOND SUTRA: A Mahayana sutra dating back to perhaps the first century expressing the concept of non-attachment.

DOKUSAN: In Zen Buddhism, an interview with the teacher or master.

EARTHLY DESIRES ARE ENLIGHTENMENT: The concept espoused by Nichiren and, in general, by Mahayana Buddhism, which holds that earthly desires do not have to be suppressed in order to attain enlightenment.

EIGHTFOLD PATH: An early teaching of Shakyamuni setting forth the principles for attaining enlightenment.

ENLIGHTENMENT: Also referred to as Buddhahood, the highest state of life, one that is free from delusion and fear.

ESHO FUNI: Expressing the concept of nonduality, the principle that life and its environment, although seemingly separate, are two phases of a single reality.

FLOWER SERMON: A Zen story about the silent transmission of enlightenment by Shakyamuni to his disciple Mahakasyapa by wordlessly handing him a flower.

FOUR NOBLE TRUTHS: A central teaching of Buddhism pertaining to the nature of suffering.

GELUK: A branch of Tibetan Buddhism. The Dalai Lama is the spiritual leader of this school.

GOHONZON: The mandala worshipped by Soka Gakkai members. The original Dai-Gohonzon was inscribed by Nichiren.

GONGYO: The liturgy chanted by Soka Gakkai members consisting of portions of two chapters of the Lotus Sutra.

GOSHO: The collected writings of Nichiren.

GREAT CONCENTRATION AND INSIGHT: A scholarly work by Zhiyi setting forth the concepts of the Ten Worlds and Three Thousand Realms in a Single Life Moment.

GROUND LUMINOSITY: According to Tibetan Buddhism, our original Buddha nature that becomes apparent at the moment of death.

GURU: A teacher in Tibetan Buddhism.

GURU YOGA: A tantric practice whereby a student unites his or her mind with that of the guru.

HEART SUTRA: A Mahayana sutra dating from the first century that describes the experience of liberation as a result of insight gained while meditating.

HENDOKU IYAKU: Literally meaning "change poison, make medicine," it stands for the fact that suffering can be transformed into benefit and enlightenment by virtue of the power of the Law.

HINAYANA: The oldest school of Buddhism, a version of which is still practiced throughout Southeast Asia. Contemporaneous Theravada practices are related to the original Hinayana texts.

ITAI DOSHIN: A concept referred to by Nichiren meaning "many in body, one in mind," or "different in body, same in spirit," suggesting that unity in a sangha can be achieved whereby a group of unique individuals share the same goal or commitment to the dharma.

KAGYU: A branch of Tibetan Buddhism.

KARMA: The repository of all of a person's causes, thoughts, and acts in the past or present that manifest themselves as various effects, correspondingly good or bad, in the present or future.

KOAN: A seemingly irrational or unanswerable riddle, parable, or story contemplated by Zen Buddhist practitioners to assist toward the realization of enlightenment.

KOSEN-RUFU: A term from the Lotus Sutra that means to declare and spread widely. Its connotation today, as used by the Soka Gakkai, generally indicates the establishment of world peace.

KYOCHI MYOGO: The fusion of reality and wisdom that occurs when chanting *Nam-myoho-renge-kyo* to a Gohonzon.

LAMA: A Tibetan teacher of the dharma.

LAMRIM: A Tibetan Buddhist text that presents the stages on the path to enlightenment.

LOTUS SUTRA: One of Shakyamuni's final teachings upon which the Tendai, Nichiren, and Soka Gakkai schools of Buddhism are based.

MAHAMUDRA: A Tibetan Buddhist meditation method focusing on the nature of the mind.

MAHA-PARINIBBANA SUTTA: A Theravada Buddhist text somewhat related to the Nirvana Sutra and concerning the end of Shakyamuni's life.

MAHAYANA: One of the two main existing branches of Buddhism, including, among others, the Zen, Nichiren, Soka Gakkai, and, in part, Tibetan Buddhist schools.

MANDALA: An object of workshop or veneration upon which Buddhists meditate or to which they chant.

MANTRA: A sound, word, or group of words that are considered to stimulate spiritual transformations. *Nam-myoho-renge-kyo* is an example of a mantra.

MERIT: In Tibetan Buddhism, that which accumulates as a result of good thoughts, deeds, or actions.

MIDDLE WAY: Also referred to as Middle Path, a Mahayana concept indicating a way or path that transcends dramatic extremes.

MUDRA: A specific hand gesture utilized during meditation practice.

NAM-MYOHO-RENGE-KYO: Literally Devotion to the Mystic Law of the Lotus Sutra, it is the mantra chanted by Soka Gakkai members, among others.

NAROPA UNIVERSITY: A fully accredited, nonsectarian university in Boulder, Colorado, founded in 1974 by Chogyam Trungpa Rinpoche and inspired by Buddhist values.

NICHIREN SHOSHU: A monastic order in Japan that in 1991 excommunicated the entire worldwide membership of the Soka Gakkai.

NIRVANA: An imperturbable state of bliss in which all suffering has been extinguished.

NIRVANA SUTRA: Generally, the Mahayana version of the sutra concerning the end of Shakyamuni's life and his teachings on eternal true self and Buddha nature. The Maha Parinibbana Sutta is the Theravada-Pali Canon version of this text.

NINE CONSCIOUSNESSES: A Buddhist concept describing nine states of consciousness inherent in every individual. The first five correspond to the five senses of sight, hearing, smell, taste, and touch. The sixth consciousness is the commonly understood conscious mind; the seventh is the inner spiritual world, including attachment to the self and the ability to recognize good and evil; the eighth consciousness is essentially what is commonly understood to be the unconscious or subconscious; and the deepest, ninth consciousness is a fundamental pure consciousness free from all karmic impurity.

NYINGMA: A branch of Tibetan Buddhism.

PURE LAND: Also known as Nembutsu, a Japanese Buddhist sect devoted to a deity called Amida Buddha, which promises heaven after death.

RINPOCHE: An honorific used in Tibetan Buddhism meaning "precious one."

RINZAI: One of the three main schools of Zen Buddhism, founded in the twelfth century by Eisai and revived in the eighteenth century by Hakuin.

RISSHO ANKOKU RON: A treatise written in 1260 by Nichiren and delivered to the Regent warning, among other things, of natural calamities and a foreign invasion of Japan unless the country's rulers took faith in his true Buddhism. The Regent declined, and Nichiren thereafter was subjected by the Regency to numerous persecutions. Subsequently, the Mongols under Kublai Khan twice attempted large-scale military invasions of Japan in 1274 and 1281.

SANGHA: A community of Buddhist believers sharing the same dharma.

SAKYA: A branch of Tibetan Buddhism.

SAMSARA: In Tibetan Buddhism, the repeating cycle of birth, life, death, and rebirth.

SATORI: In Zen Buddhism, a state of enlightenment, or the awakening through zazen meditation to one's true nature.

SHAKUBUKU: A term meaning proselytization commonly referred to in the Soka Gakkai community.

SHAMBHALA: A legendary, mystical pure land of Tibetan Buddhism, as well as the namesake for meditation centers established throughout North America by Chogyam Trungpa Rinpoche.

SHINGON: A Buddhist school in Japan based in part on Vajrayana teachings.

SHOTEN ZENJIN: Heavenly beings or protective functions in the universe said to protect those who correctly practice Buddhism.

SIX PARAMITAS: The perfection or culmination of six certain virtues.

SIX YOGAS OF NAROPA: In Tibetan Buddhism, six practices intended to help in the achievement of enlightenment.

SOKA UNIVERSITY OF AMERICA: A fully accredited, nonsectarian university in Aliso Viejo, California, founded by Daisaku Ikeda and inspired by the values of peace, human rights, and the sanctity of life

SOTO: The largest of the three main schools of Zen, established in Japan by Master Dogen in the thirteenth century.

TANTRA: Vajrayana methods of meditation employed by Tibetan Buddhists.

TENDAI: A Buddhist sect in Japan (originally founded in China) inspired by Zhiyi's teachings and the Lotus Sutra.

TEN PRECEPTS: A set of ten Buddhist principles of morality intended for novice monks or practitioners to follow.

TEN WORLDS: A theory of life set forth by Zhiyi, based on the Lotus Sutra.

THERAVADA: A major school of Buddhism based largely on what was historically referred to as Hinayana teachings.

THREE JEWELS: The three most important constituent elements of Buddhism: the Buddha, the dharma, and the sangha.

THREE POISONS: The fundamental evils inherent in life and that cause delusion, usually referred to as greed, anger, and ignorance.

TONGLEN: In Tibetan Buddhism, a method of meditation meant to relieve the suffering of others.

TULKU: In Tibetan Buddhism, a person recognized as a reincarnation of a past master.

VAJRAYANA: A complex system of tantric Buddhist practice, based on both Theravada and Mahayana principles, and which includes Tibetan Buddhism.

VINAYA: Traditional rules set forth for Buddhist monastics strictly prescribing aspects of their daily lives, including prayer, study, work, and sexual and dietary habits.

WRATHFUL DEITIES: In Tibetan Buddhism, enlightened beings who take on wrathful forms to help lead practitioners to enlightenment.

ZAZEN: The method of meditation in Zen Buddhism.

ZHINAY: A method of meditation in Tibetan Buddhism.

ZUIHO BINI: A Buddhist precept indicating that, in matters the Buddha did not expressly either permit or forbid, one may act in accordance with local custom so long as the fundamental principles of Buddhism are not violated.

Acknowledgments

My thanks to Holly Rubino, my charming, meticulous, and encouraging editor; Jennifer Lyons, my brilliant colleague and literary agent; and Daniel Hess, who lovingly showed me his beautiful town of Boulder and opened many doors for me when I was there. I further thank the following individuals who generously offered their time and assistance: Geoffrey Shugen Arnold, David Bartolomi, John Cobb, Barbara Dilley, Peter, Sara, and Asher Dwoskin, Rosine Mbango, Suzie Sarif, and Lisa Trank. All the good stuff herein is thanks to them, and any mistakes are mine alone.

I'm also grateful to my mother and father for giving me this life, and to my wife, Jessica, and our three sons, Jake, Kevin, and Vince, who make it so worth living.

Finally, I wish to acknowledge the efforts on my behalf of Danny Nagashima, without which this book would never have been written.

Index